S•O•U•P•S
FOR ALL
SEASONS

Also by Nava Atlas

VEGETARIANA

AMERICAN HARVEST

THE WHOLEFOOD CATALOG

VEGETARIAN CELEBRATIONS

S·O·U·P·S

FOR ALL

SEASONS

Bountiful Vegetarian Soups

Written and illustrated by

NAVA ATLAS

Amberwood Press
New Paltz, NY

I'd like to thank the following contributors for their tasty soup recipes: Toni Atlas for Morroccan-Style Vegetable Soup, Commander's Palace restaurant in New Orleans for Creole Eggplant Soup, Gary Raheb in memory of his mother, Grace Raheb, for Cream of Lettuce Soup, and Neil Trager for Hot-and-Sour Oriental Vegetable Soup. I'd also like to acknowledge the technical support of Gil Plantinga, who made doing this book possible at an impossible time in my life.

SOUPS FOR ALL SEASONS
Bountiful Vegetarian Soups
Copyright © 1992 by Nava Atlas
Cover and text design by Nava Atlas

Publisher's Cataloging in Publication
(Prepared by Quality Books Inc.)

Atlas, Nava
    Soups for all seasons : bountiful vegetarian soups/
Nava Atlas
    p. cm.
    Includes index.
    ISBN 0-9630243-1-0

    1. Vegetarian cookery.   2. Soups.   I. Title.   II. Title:
Bountiful Vegetarian Soups.

TX837.A8 1992   641.563'6
                                        QBI92-991

Printed in the United States of America
10 9 8 7 6 5 4 3

CONTENTS

INTRODUCTION

Soups have always held a very prominent spot in my culinary repertoire. I regard them as one of the most rewarding, yet at the same time, one of the easiest things a cook can prepare. Within this category of cookery exists the widest range of possibilities and results—a soup might be familiar and soothing, evoking memories of the warmth and comfort of a childhood home, or it might be a mélange of sophisticated flavors that meld together in a pleasingly unexpected way.

Best of all, soups are welcome at any time of year, reflecting the harvest of each season. A soup can transform the lush diversity of summer's fruits and vegetables into a most refreshing and appetizing elixir. Few dishes can ease the humdrum of winter's homely foods like a bowl of hot soup. And the tender new produce of spring and the bounty of fall's harvest are used to good advantage as part of a savory concoction served in a bowl.

The soups presented here are in keeping with today's emphasis on low-fat, high-fiber foods. Along with seasonal produce, you will find within these recipes a wide variety of whole grains and legumes. For ease of selection, I've organized the soups into chapters reflecting the four seasons. And while you will find it convenient to have stick-to-the-ribs soups grouped together in the winter section, cold soups in the summer section, and so on, many of the soups are seasonally interchangeable. This is especially the case with the fall and spring sections—there is no reason you can't have Chick-Pea and Tahini Soup in the spring or White Bean Purée with Zucchini and Herbs in the fall.

It almost goes without saying that you need not be a vegetarian to enjoy meatless soups—with inspiration coming from around the globe, they are for everyone that loves the melding of flavorful ingredients, and the wonderful aromas that a big pot of simmering soup imparts like nothing else can.

COOKING NOTES

EQUIPMENT

The soups in this book are simple enough to require only the most basic of kitchen equipment. Aside from a good, heavy soup pot or Dutch oven, of course, the items needed are standard to most any kitchen: wooden spoons for stirring, a colander for washing leeks and leafy vegetables, a grater, measuring utensils, and good knives. For the devoted soup cook, I heartily recommend a blender or food processor for puréed soups; the food processor is also useful for making occasional grating easier and quicker.

FREEZING

Some soups freeze well, but others lose much of their flavor and texture. Thick winter bean and grain soups do well, as do simple broths and stocks. Freezing often changes the texture of a smooth purée, making it more watery. Avoid freezing soups that contain potatoes or lentils, both of which turn quite mushy. Also to be avoided— freezing soups containing raw ingredients, as in certain chilled soups. Most soups given here do not produce such enormous quantities as to warrant long-term storage of leftovers, as I generally prefer finishing a soup while it's fresh rather than after it's been frozen and thawed.

SOUP TEXTURES AND CONSISTENCIES

Here is an area that is rarely discussed in the presentation of soup recipes, and yet is almost as important to tailor to the individual recipe as is seasoning. Soup-making, though essentially very simple, is an inexact science. For instance, what one cook considers a large potato might be a medium one to another, and so the amount of water or liquid called for in a recipe might not always yield precise results. The soup recipes here often remind the cook to adjust the consistency, or thickness, and this, like salting, should be done according to the cook's preference. Some soups are meant to be very thick, and others to be thin and brothy, but most seem to fall somewhere in between, and thus may be tailored to one's liking.

SEASONINGS FOR SOUPS

All soups benefit from just the right balance of seasoning, to lend depth of flavor. Predictably, this is particularly true for vegetarian soups, where even the use of a good vegetable stock may not be all it takes to create a complete, full-bodied flavor. Using an interesting mix of flavorings, adding dried herbs and ground spices early in the cooking, and tasting often to adjust those seasonings, all contribute to the success of a vegetarian soup. Quantities of seasonings given in soup recipes—in this book and elsewhere—should be tailored to individual tastes.

As a perennial soup enthusiast, I have always loved to experiment with a pinch of this spice, a quarter teaspoon of this herb, and a half teaspoon of that. That's part of the fun and artistry of making soup. After motherhood intervened, I enjoyed the practicality of making a big pot of soup that would last several days, but I began leaning toward recipes that could be made simply and quickly. The best time-saver I discovered was eliminating the need for measuring minute quantities of herbs and spices, and instead using purchased seasoning mixes.

There are many blends and brands around, and they are wonderfully suited to use in soups, where small quantities of many seasonings add up to the zing needed to make a meatless soup taste great. Feel free to experiment with the many varieties available. Here are the types of mixes I use most often in making soups:

Curry powder (good quality) or *garam masala*: Purchase this blend from a spice shop, natural food store, or Indian grocery. Use your sense of smell—it should be fragrant and pungent. The curry powder sold in supermarkets falls short; it's too flat and bland.

Italian herb seasoning mix: A blend of several of the following herbs—oregano, thyme, marjoram, rosemary, dill.

Salt-free herb-and-spice seasoning mix: The savory blend of many different herbs and spices eliminates the need for excess salt. This is an all-purpose way to add zest to many soups. There are several good brands available in supermarkets and natural food stores.

Lemon-pepper: The use of this mix is a pleasant way to give a lemony bite to Oriental soups and vegetable purées. Available in several brands in supermarkets and through spice outlets.

Here are some final seasoning tips:

• Add salt toward the end of the cooking, to give the other flavors a chance to develop and thus avoid oversalting. Salt a little at a time, stir in thoroughly, and taste frequently.

• For those who need to limit their intake of salt, try adding lemon juice for added zest.

• A small amount of dry wine adds nice depth of flavor. I use wine in some of the soups, but readers might like to experiment with it wherever they feel appropriate.

STOCKS AND BROTHS

The absence of a strong-flavored meat stock makes the preparation of tasty meatless soups a challenge, but honestly, not a very difficult one. Many ethnic cuisines produce classic soups which in their intrinsic form are completely vegetarian. True, almost any soup can benefit from a good stock to really round out its flavor, but I place fresh and flavorful ingredients and creative seasoning above stocks in contributing to the success of a soup. I would venture to say that at least 90 percent of the soup recipes in this book will work as well using plain water as they will with a stock; still, it's useful to have stocks on hand when they're needed, and to have a few basic recipes to refer to.

Following are a handful of stocks and broths, the first two of which are suitable as soup bases. The remaining ones, in the Oriental tradition, make good broths to be eaten on their own or lightly embellished.

LIGHT VEGETABLE STOCK

Makes about 6 cups

This is a basic stock that may be used in place of water in most any vegetable soup to give added depth of flavor. It's also a good way to use up vegetables that are limp or less than perfectly fresh.

7 cups water
1 large onion, chopped
1 large carrot, sliced
2 large celery stalks, sliced
1 medium potato, scrubbed and diced
1 cup coarsely shredded white cabbage
1 teaspoon salt
2 teaspoons Italian herb seasoning mix

Place all the ingredients in a large soup pot. Bring to a boil, then simmer, covered, over low heat for 40 to 45 minutes, or until the vegetables are quite tender. Strain the stock through 3 layers of cheesecloth.

ONION OR LEEK AND GARLIC BROTH

Makes about 6 cups

This broth may be used as an extra-flavorful soup stock, or as an alternative, with a little extra kick, to Light Vegetable Stock (page 10). It's also a soothing remedy for the common cold!

1 tablespoon margarine
1 large onion, chopped, or 2 medium leeks,
   white parts only, cut into ¼-inch rings
4 to 6 cloves garlic, minced
6 cups water
¼ cup dry red wine
1 teaspoon salt
⅛ teaspoon freshly ground pepper, optional

Heat the margarine in a large heavy saucepan. If using leeks, separate the rings and rinse them well to remove grit. Add the onion or leeks and sauté over moderate heat until golden. Add the garlic and continue to sauté until the onion or leeks brown lightly. Add the water, wine, salt, and optional pepper, and bring to a boil. Cover and simmer over low heat for 30 to 40 minutes. You may leave the onions and garlic in, if you wish, or strain the stock through a fine sieve or cheesecloth.

SIMPLE MISO BROTH

Makes about 6 cups

Miso is a nutritious, high-protein product fermented from soybeans and salt (or a combination of soybeans, grains, and salt). With a consistency similar to a nut-butter, pungent-tasting misos are quite commonly found in natural food stores and Oriental groceries, which is also where you'll find the kombu needed for this broth. A traditional Japanese food, miso is most commonly used to make simple broths which are enjoyed in Japan at any time of day—even at breakfast. Here is a basic recipe, which really should be considered a soup in itself, rather than as a stock for making other soups. Note that once the miso is stirred into water, it should not be boiled, otherwise its beneficial enzymes will be destroyed.

6 cups water
2 strips of kombu (sea vegetable), each 3 by 5 inches
2 to 4 tablespoons miso, to taste

Combine the water and kombu in a soup pot and bring to a boil. Remove the kombu. Dissolve the desired amount of miso in just enough warm water to make it pourable. Stir into the broth and remove from the heat. Serve at once.

Embellishments for miso broth (any combination of the following):
• Diced tofu (bean curd)
• Cooked Oriental noodles
• Finely chopped spring onions
• Grated fresh daikon radish or white turnip
• Grated crisp cucumber

BASIC DASHI
(Japanese Kombu and Shiitake Mushroom Broth)
Makes about 6 cups

Along with miso broth, *dashi* is another traditional Japanese stock that may be embellished in a number of ways, or eaten very simply. It also makes a good base for certain Oriental vegetable soups. Look for the sea vegetable kombu and dried shiitake mushrooms in Oriental groceries or in natural food stores.

6 cups water
2 strips of kombu (sea vegetable), each
**   about 3 by 7 inches**
6 to 8 dried shiitake mushrooms

Combine the water and kombu in a soup pot. Bring to a boil, then remove the kombu. Add the mushrooms to the stock and remove from the heat. Let stand for 30 minutes. Remove the mushrooms from the stock with a slotted spoon. Trim them of their tough stems, and save them for another use, or slice them and use them in the broth.

Variations:
DASHI WITH NOODLES: Simply cook a quantity of Oriental noodles in the stock. Once they are *al dente,* remove the soup from the heat, season to taste with natural soy sauce, and serve immediately. Garnish each serving with some finely chopped scallion.

DASHI WITH MISO AND VEGETABLES: Use the broth to simmer any quantity of thinly sliced vegetables such as carrot, cabbage, daikon radish, turnip, etc. Once the vegetables are just done, add 2 to 4 tablespoons of miso, to taste, dissolved in just enough warm water to make it pourable. Stir in the sliced shiitake mushrooms from the preparation of the stock. Remove from the heat and serve at once.

ORIENTAL MUSHROOM BROTH

Makes about 6 cups

Of the Oriental stocks and broths given here, this is the strongest-flavored. It is most appropriate to use in Chinese-style vegetable soups, but is also a very pleasing broth to be eaten on its own. You may use embellishments as given under Simple Miso Broth (page 12).

2 teaspoons sesame oil
1 small onion, minced
1 clove garlic, minced
6 cups water
8 to 10 dried shiitake mushrooms
1 to 2 tablespoons natural soy sauce, to taste

Heat the oil in a large, heavy saucepan. Add the onion and garlic and sauté over moderately low heat until the onion is golden. Add the water, mushrooms, and soy sauce. Bring to a boil, then cover and simmer over low heat for 15 minutes. Remove from the heat and let stand another 15 minutes. Strain through a fine sieve. Reserve the mushrooms, trimming them first of their tough stems. Save them for another use, or slice them and return them to the broth.

F•A•L•L

Autumn is an inviting time to make soup. In early to mid-season, the colors and rich flavors of the harvest can be shown off to great advantage in a warm tureen of soup. Later in the season, the primary function of a hot bowl of soup is to counteract the effects of the onset of chilly weather.

BAKED ONION SOUP

6 servings

Ceramic crocks with handles are the ideal bowls for this soup, but any type of ovenproof bowl will do. Miso makes a robust base for this classic soup, in place of the customary meat stock. For more on miso, see page 12, under Simple Miso Broth.

2½ tablespoons safflower oil
8 medium onions, quartered and thinly sliced
2 cloves garlic, minced
⅓ cup dry red wine
1 teaspoon dry mustard
2 to 4 tablespoons miso, to taste,
    dissolved in ⅓ cup water (see note below)
French bread as needed
½ pound grated mozzarella cheese or
    mozzarella-style soy cheese

Heat the oil in a large soup pot. Add the onions and sauté over low heat until golden. Add the garlic and continue to sauté slowly until the onions are evenly browned. Add 5 cups water, wine, and mustard. Bring to a boil, then simmer over low heat, covered, for 15 minutes. Stir in the dissolved miso and remove from the heat. Allow the soup to stand for another 15 minutes.

In the meantime, slice the bread into 1-inch-thick slices, allowing 1 slice per serving. Bake in a preheated, 350-degree oven for 15 to 20 minutes, or until dry and crisp.

To assemble the soup, place a slice of bread into each ovenproof bowl and ladle a serving of soup over it. Sprinkle the cheese over the tops. Place the bowls on 1 or 2 cookie sheets so that they will be easier to handle. Bake the soup for approximately 10 minutes, or until the cheese is thoroughly melted. Serve at once.

Note: If you are unfamiliar with the intensity of the flavor of miso, you might want to start with only 2 tablespoons, dissolved in half the water recommended above. Taste the soup, then add more dissolved miso to your taste if you'd like a stronger flavor.

"Onion: humble kindred of the lily clan, rooted from oblivion by Alexander the Great and bestrewn by him, along with learning, to the civilised world, thus lending a touch of wisdom and sophistication to the whole."

—Della Lutes
The Country Kitchen, 1938

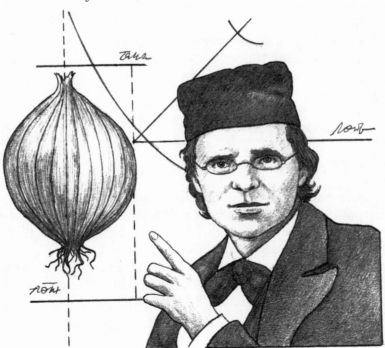

JERUSALEM ARTICHOKE PURÉE WITH LEEKS

6 to 8 servings

Jerusalem artichokes have a unique flavor and texture (something of a cross between potatoes and water chestnuts) that is savored by some, and considered somewhat peculiar by others. If you belong to the former group, or if you are simply adventurous, you are likely to enjoy this offbeat soup. Barley or Rice Triangles (page 113) complement it nicely.

1½ pounds Jerusalem artichokes, scrubbed and diced
2 medium potatoes, peeled and diced
1 large onion, chopped
¼ cup white wine
½ teaspoon good-quality curry powder or *garam masala*
Light Vegetable Stock (page 10),
    or water with 1 vegetable bouillon cube
2 large leeks
2 tablespoons margarine
3 tablespoons minced fresh parsley
Juice of ½ lemon
Salt and freshly ground pepper to taste

Reserve and set aside about ⅓ of the diced Jerusalem artichokes. Place the rest in a large soup pot along with the potatoes, onion, wine, and curry powder, and just enough water or stock to barely cover the vegetables. Bring to a boil, then cover and simmer until the vegetables are tender, about 20 minutes.

Purée the soup in batches in a food processor or blender, then return to the soup pot. Add additional water or stock if the soup is too thick, just enough to achieve a smooth and medium-thick consistency. Return to low heat.

Cut the leeks into ¼-inch slices. Remove and discard the tough green leaves. Separate the rings of the leeks and rinse well to remove grit. Heat the margarine in a skillet. Add the leeks and reserved artichoke dice and sauté over moderate heat until both are just beginning to brown lightly. Stir into the soup, along with the parsley and lemon juice, and season to taste with salt and pepper. If time allows, let the soup stand for an hour or so before serving, then heat through as needed.

As often as you have eaten the strong-smelling shoots of Tarentine leeks, give kisses with shut mouth.

—Martial (c. A.D. 40-104)
  Epigrams

GINGERED PUMPKIN-APPLE SOUP

6 to 8 servings

Make this soup a day ahead, if you can. The unusual combination of flavors benefit from having time to blend.

(oil)
2 tablespoons margarine
1 large onion, finely chopped
2 medium celery stalks, finely diced
2 medium tart apples, peeled, cored, and diced
4 cups Light Vegetable Stock (page 10) or water
l-pound can unsweetened pumpkin purée
1 teaspoon grated fresh ginger
1 teaspoon good-quality curry powder or *garam masala*
½ teaspoon cinnamon
¼ teaspoon nutmeg
2 cups low-fat milk or soymilk, or as needed
Salt to taste
Chopped almonds or cashews for garnish

(oil)
Heat the margarine in a large soup pot. Add the onion and celery and sauté until the onion is golden. Add the remaining ingredients except for the last 3. Bring to a boil, then simmer over low heat, covered, for 35 to 40 minutes. Stir in enough milk or soymilk to achieve a smooth and slightly thick consistency. Season to taste with salt. Remove from heat.

Allow the soup to stand overnight or for several hours to develop flavor. Taste and add more seasonings if desired. Heat through as needed when ready to serve. Garnish each serving with a handful of chopped almonds or cashews.

MORROCCAN-STYLE VEGETABLE SOUP

6 or more servings

This delicious soup looks and smells as enticing as it tastes.

2 tablespoons safflower oil
2 large onions, chopped
2 medium potatoes, scrubbed and cut into ¾-inch chunks
2 heaping cups raw pumpkin or butternut squash,
  peeled and cut into ¾-inch chunks
2 large carrots, coarsely chopped
14-ounce can plum tomatoes with liquid, chopped
2 teaspoons ground cumin
¾ teaspoon turmeric
2 cups well-cooked or canned chick-peas
Salt and freshly ground pepper to taste
1 cup couscous (see note)

Heat the oil in a large soup pot. Add the onions and sauté over moderate heat until golden. Add the potatoes, pumpkin or squash, carrots, tomatoes, and enough water to cover. Bring to a boil, then add the seasonings and simmer over low heat, covered, for approximately 45 minutes, or until the vegetables are tender. Add the chick-peas, and season to taste with salt and pepper. Simmer over very low heat for another 15 minutes.

In the meantime, place the couscous in an ovenproof bowl. Cover with 2 cups of boiling water, then cover the bowl and let stand for 15 minutes. Fluff with a fork. Place a small amount of the couscous in each soup bowl, then ladle the soup over it. Serve at once.

Note: The couscous referred to here is presteamed, cracked semolina, available in natural food stores. Look for the whole-grain variety, which is a soft tan color rather than yellowish, as the refined type is.

CHICK-PEA AND TAHINI SOUP

6 servings

The classic Middle Eastern team of chick-peas and tahini (sesame paste, available in natural food stores and Middle Eastern specialty groceries) is combined here in an offbeat, nontraditional soup. Serve with fresh whole wheat pita bread. Middle Eastern bulgur salad, tabouli, would round this meal out completely. Recipes for tabouli can be found in many vegetarian and Middle Eastern cookbooks.

1 tablespoon olive oil
3 to 4 cloves garlic, minced
5 cups Light Vegetable Stock (page 10),
    Onion or Leek and Garlic Broth (page 11),
    or cooking liquid from the chick-peas
2 cups mushrooms, coarsely chopped
1 cup finely shredded white cabbage
1 bay leaf
1 teaspoon ground cumin
2 teaspoons salt-free herb-and-spice seasoning mix
5 cups canned or well-cooked chick-peas
    (from about 1 pound dry chick-peas)
⅓ cup tahini
¼ cup finely chopped fresh parsley
3 to 4 scallions, green parts only,
    sliced into fine rounds
2 tablespoons minced fresh dill
Juice of ½ to 1 lemon, to taste
Salt and freshly ground pepper to taste

    Heat the olive oil in a large soup pot. Add the garlic and sauté over low heat for 1 minute.

    Add the liquid, mushrooms, cabbage, bay leaf, and seasonings. Bring to a boil, then simmer, covered, over low heat for 15 minutes.

In the meantime, place about ¾ of the chick-peas in the container of a food processor or blender with the tahini. Set the rest of the chick-peas aside. Process until very smoothly puréed. Stir the purée into the soup pot slowly, until well blended with the liquid. Stir in the reserved chick-peas, bring to a simmer, and cook over very low heat for 10 minutes. Add the remaining ingredients and correct the consistency if necessary with more stock or water. Season to taste with salt and pepper, then simmer for another 10 minutes.

Chick-peas are under the dominion of Venus. They are less windy than beans, but nourish more...they have a cleansing facility.

—Nicolas Culpeper (1616-1654)
  Culpeper's Complete Herbal

ALMOND BRUSSELS SPROUTS SOUP

Serves 6

Elegant and highly flavored, this soup features protein-rich almonds as its base. A fresh loaf of whole wheat bread, and a salad featuring tomatoes and strong greens make excellent companions.

1 cup toasted almonds
2½ tablespoons safflower oil, divided
1 large onion, chopped
1 large celery stalk, chopped
1 clove garlic, minced
1 large potato, peeled and diced
⅓ cup dry white wine
1 large tomato, diced
1½ pounds Brussels sprouts, trimmed
   and coarsely chopped
2½ teaspoons salt-free herb-and-spice seasoning mix
1 to 2 tablespoons lemon juice, or to taste
Salt and freshly ground pepper to taste
Slivered or chopped almonds for garnish
Chopped fresh parsley for garnish

Place the almonds in the container of a food processor or blender. Process until very finely ground. Add 1 tablespoon of the oil and continue to process until the mixture resembles a nut butter. Stop the machine and scrape down the sides with a plastic spatula from time to time, if necessary.

Heat the remaining oil in a large soup pot. Add the onion and sauté until it is golden. Add the celery, garlic, potato, wine, tomato, and about two-thirds of the Brussels sprouts (reserve and set aside the remainder). Add enough water to barely cover the vegetables. Bring to a boil, and add the almond butter and seasoning mix. Simmer, covered, over low heat for 35 to 40 minutes, or until all the vegetables are tender. Remove from the heat.

Transfer the solid ingredients to a food processor or blender and purée in batches. Return to the soup pot over very low heat. Thin with a small amount of water if the soup is too thick.

In a separate saucepan, steam the reserved Brussels sprouts in about ½ inch of water until they are bright green and tender-crisp. Add them to the soup along with the lemon juice, and salt and pepper to taste. Serve the soup at once, or allow to stand for an hour or so before serving, then heat through as needed. Garnish each serving with some chopped or slivered almonds and fresh parsley.

BROCCOLI, APPLE, AND PEANUT SOUP

6 to 8 servings

Though admittedly rich, with a generous amount of peanut butter, this soup has an unusual and luscious flavor.

2 tablespoons margarine
2 large onions, chopped
2 cloves garlic, minced
3 medium carrots, sliced
3 heaping cups finely chopped broccoli
2 medium apples, peeled, cored, and diced
6 cups Light Vegetable Stock (page 10) or water
¼ cup dry white wine
1 teaspoon good-quality curry powder or *garam masala*
⅔ cup natural peanut butter
Juice of ½ lemon
Salt to taste
Chopped roasted peanuts for garnish

Heat the margarine in a large soup pot. Add the onions and garlic and sauté over moderate heat until the onions are golden.

Set aside about ⅓ of the carrot slices and about 1 heaping cup of broccoli florets. Place the rest of the carrots and broccoli in the soup pot along with the apple, water or stock, wine, and seasoning. Bring to a boil, then cover and simmer over low heat until the carrots and broccoli are tender, about 20 minutes. Remove from the heat.

Transfer the solid ingredients from the soup to the container of a food processor or blender with a slotted spoon, about half at a time. Purée each batch with about half of the peanut butter. Stir the purée back into the soup stock in the pot. If the soup is too thick, add enough additional water or stock to achieve a medium-thick consistency. Return to low heat and simmer for 10 minutes.

In the meantime, steam the reserved carrots in a heavy saucepan with about ¼ cup water, covered, for 5 minutes. Add the reserved broccoli florets and steam for another 5 minutes, just until both are brightly colored and tender-crisp. Stir into the soup along with the lemon juice. Season to taste with salt and remove from the heat. Garnish each serving with a handful of chopped peanuts.

Never blow your soup if it is too hot, but wait until it cools. Never raise your plate to your lips, but eat it with your spoon.

—C.B. Hartley
The Gentleman's Book of Etiquette, 1873

This gentleman eats his soup properly, but his posture is abominable, and his hat is on.

This gentleman's posture is excellent, but he eats his soup in a shockingly rude fashion.

GARLICKY CREAM OF CELERY SOUP

6 servings

This smooth soup will win you over with its elegant simplicity and intense celery flavor. Nothing enhances it better than Garlic Croutons (page 121).

12 large celery stalks
2 tablespoons margarine, divided
1 large onion, chopped
8 cloves garlic, minced
2 tablespoons unbleached white flour
3 medium potatoes, peeled and diced
2 teaspoons salt-free herb-and-spice seasoning mix
¼ cup mixed chopped fresh parsley and dill
¼ cup celery leaves
1 to 1½ cups low-fat milk or soymilk, as needed
Salt and freshly ground pepper to taste
Chopped fresh dill or parsley for garnish

Trim 10 stalks of celery and cut them into ½-inch dice. Trim the remaining 2 stalks, cut them into ¼-inch dice, and set aside.

Heat a tablespoon of the margarine in a large soup pot. Add the onion and garlic and sauté over moderate heat until the onion is lightly golden. Sprinkle in the flour and stir it in until it disappears. Add the 10 stalks of celery, the potatoes, and just enough water to cover. Bring to a boil, then add the seasoning mix, fresh herbs, and celery leaves. Simmer over low heat until the vegetables are tender, about 25 minutes. Remove from the heat.

With a slotted spoon, transfer the solid ingredients to the container of a food processor or blender and purée, in batches if necessary, until very smooth. Stir back into the soup pot. Return to very low heat and add enough milk or soymilk to achieve a slightly thick consistency.

Heat the remaining margarine in a small skillet. Add the reserved celery and sauté over moderate heat until it is touched with golden spots. Add to the soup, then season to taste with salt and pepper. Serve at once, or allow the soup to stand for an hour or so, then heat through as needed. Garnish each serving with chopped dill or parsley.

Last night with the celery, autumn came into its own. There is a crispness about celery that is the essence of October. It is as fresh and clean as a rainy day after a spell of heat...

—A.A. Milne
  Not That It Matters, 1920

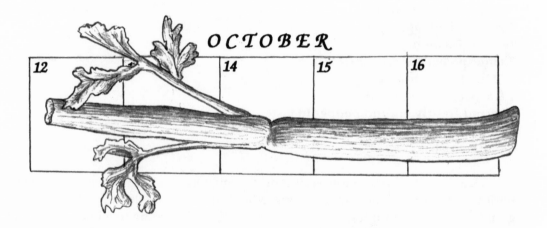

HOT BEET AND POTATO BORSCHT

6 to 8 servings

Though beet borscht is generally eaten cold, the addition of potatoes creates a more robust version for fall or winter. Onion-Rye Oven Scones (page 116) complement this soup well.

2 tablespoons safflower oil
2 large onions, chopped
3 medium potatoes, peeled and grated
4 medium beets, peeled and grated
1 large carrot, grated
1 medium celery stalk, finely diced
Handful of celery leaves
1 cup fresh orange juice
Juice of 1 lemon
2 tablespoons minced fresh dill, or
    2 teaspoons dried dill
1 teaspoon dry mustard
Salt and freshly ground pepper to taste
Sour cream or plain yogurt, or a combination,
    for garnish

Heat the oil in a large soup pot. Add the onions and sauté over moderate heat until golden. Add all the remaining ingredients except the salt and pepper and the garnish, and add enough water to cover the vegetables. Bring to a boil, then cover and simmer over low heat until the vegetables are tender, about 40 to 45 minutes. Adjust the consistency with more water if the soup is crowded. Season to taste with salt and pepper.

Allow the soup to stand for an hour or so before serving, then heat through as needed. Ladle the soup into bowls, and garnish each serving with a small scoop of sour cream, yogurt, or a combination of the two.

SWEET POTATO SOUP

Serves 6

A warming soup with an appealing golden color, the natural sweetness of the sweet potatoes gives this soup a surprising flavor twist.

2 tablespoons margarine
2 medium onions, chopped
2 medium carrots, diced
1 large celery stalk, diced
Handful of celery leaves
6 cups diced (½-inch) sweet potatoes
2 bay leaves
¼ teaspoon dried thyme
¼ teaspoon ground nutmeg
1 cup low-fat milk or soymilk, or as needed
Salt and freshly ground pepper to taste

Heat the margarine in a large soup pot. Add the onions, carrots, and celery and sauté over low heat until the onions are golden. Add the celery leaves and sweet potato dice. Add just enough water to cover all but about 1 inch of the vegetables. Bring to a boil, then stir in the bay leaves and seasonings. Simmer over moderate heat until the sweet potatoes and vegetables are tender, about 20 minutes.

With a slotted spoon, remove about half of the solid ingredients and transfer to a food processor along with about ½ cup of the cooking liquid. Process until smoothly puréed, then stir back into the soup pot. Add the milk or soymilk as needed to achieve a slightly thick consistency. Season to taste with salt and pepper. Simmer over very low heat for another 10 to 15 minutes.

POTATO, CHEESE, AND GREEN CHILI SOUP

6 servings

This flavorful soup is a contemporary classic from the American Southwest. A great soup to make in the early fall, while fresh corn and tomatoes are still available.

4 medium potatoes, peeled and diced
5 cups Light Vegetable Stock (page 10) or water
2 tablespoons safflower or olive oil
1 large onion, chopped
2 to 3 cloves garlic, crushed or minced
1 large green bell pepper, finely chopped
1 cup chopped fresh, ripe tomatoes or canned tomatoes
¾ cup cooked fresh or thawed frozen corn kernels
6-ounce can chopped mild green chili peppers
1 teaspoon chili powder
½ pound sharp Cheddar cheese or Cheddar-style
  soy cheese, grated
Salt and freshly ground pepper to taste

Place the potato dice in a large soup pot and cover with the water or vegetable stock. Bring to a boil, then cover and simmer over low heat until the potatoes are just tender, about 15 minutes.

In the meantime, heat the oil in a small skillet. Sauté the onion over low heat until it is translucent. Add the garlic and green pepper and sauté until the mixture begins to brown lightly. Remove half of the potatoes from their cooking liquid with a slotted spoon and mash well. Stir the mashed potatoes back into the soup pot along with the skillet mixture, tomatoes, corn, green chilies and chili powder. Simmer over low heat for 20 minutes.

Sprinkle in the grated cheese, just a bit at a time, stirring it in until it disappears each time. Season to taste with salt and pepper and allow the soup to simmer over very low heat, stirring frequently, for another 5 minutes.

Serve at once, or let stand for an hour or so before serving. Heat through as needed, and adjust the consistency if necessary with more water or stock if the soup becomes too thick.

To be a maker of good soups one must not only have skill and patience, but must also use good materials...Soup should be palatable and nutritious. If these qualities be lacking, there will be no excuse for serving it. Knowledge and care must be applied in combining the various ingredients in order to secure results at once pleasing and healthful.

—Maria Parloa
Miss Parloa's Kitchen Companion, 1887

SQUASH AND CORN CHOWDER

6 to 8 servings

The perfect time to make this soup is early fall, when the first squash comes to the market, and when fresh corn is still being harvested.

1 medium butternut squash (about 1½ pounds)
1 heaping cup chopped onion
1 celery stalk, finely diced
1 large sweet potato, peeled and diced
Light Vegetable Stock (page 10) or water
2 tablespoons margarine
2 bay leaves
2 teaspoons salt-free herb-and-spice seasoning mix
½ teaspoon dried thyme
2½ to 3 cups cooked fresh corn kernels
   (from about 3 medium ears)
1 cup low-fat milk or soymilk, or as needed
Salt and freshly ground pepper to taste

With a sharp knife, cut the squash across the center of the rounded part. Remove the seeds and fibers. Slice the squash into ½-inch rings, then peel each ring and chop into small dice. Place the squash dice in a large soup pot along with the chopped onion, celery, and sweet potato and add enough water or stock to cover all but about an inch of the vegetables, leaving them above water level. Bring to a boil, then add the margarine, bay leaves, and seasonings. Cover and simmer over low heat, stirring once or twice, until the squash and potatoes are tender, about 25 to 30 minutes.

With a slotted spoon, scoop out 2 heaping cups of the solid ingredients, mash them well, and stir back into the soup. Add the cooked corn kernels and enough milk or soymilk to achieve a slightly thick consistency. Season to taste with salt and pepper. Simmer over low heat for another 10 to 15 minutes. This soup may be served at once, but if time allows, let the soup stand for an hour or so before serving, then heat through as needed.

HOT SLAW SOUP

6 servings

This soup was inspired by the combination of ingredients used in the classic American salad. Cheddar-Oat Griddle Biscuits (page 114) or Cheese and Herb Corn Muffins (page 111) enhance this soup nicely.

2 tablespoons margarine
2 medium onions, grated or minced
4 cups grated or finely shredded white cabbage
2 medium carrots, grated
1 medium parsnip or white turnip, cut in ¼-inch dice
1 medium celery stalk, finely diced
Light Vegetable Stock (page 10) or water to cover
⅓ cup quick-cooking oats
2 teaspoons salt-free herb-and-spice seasoning mix
1 teaspoon dried dill
2 to 3 tablespoons apple cider vinegar, to taste
1½ to 2 cups low-fat milk or soymilk, as needed
Salt and freshly ground pepper to taste
Sour cream or yogurt, or a combination,
    for topping, optional

Heat the margarine in a large soup pot. Add the onions and sauté over moderate heat until golden. Add the cabbage, carrots, parsnip, and celery along with just enough water or stock to cover. Bring to a boil, then simmer over low heat, covered, until nearly tender, about 20 to 25 minutes. Stir in the oats, seasoning mix, dill, and vinegar, and simmer for another 10 to 15 minutes, or until the vegetables are done.

Stir in the milk or soymilk as needed, then season to taste with salt and pepper. Simmer just until the soup is heated through. If you'd like, top each serving with a small scoop of sour cream or yogurt, or a combination of both.

BLACK BEAN SOUP

6 to 8 servings

A classic American soup, this is robust and brimming with complex flavors. With any of the muffins, pages 110 to 112, and a simple salad, this soup is the basis of a filling and hearty meal.

1 pound dried black (turtle) beans
1½ tablespoons safflower oil
1 cup chopped onion
2 large carrots, chopped
2 large celery stalks, diced
2 or 3 cloves garlic, crushed or minced
3 tablespoons chopped fresh parsley
2 bay leaves
2 teaspoons salt-free herb-and-spice seasoning mix
¼ teaspoon nutmeg
¼ cup dry red wine or sherry
Salt and freshly ground pepper to taste

Garnish:
1 tablespoon margarine
1 large onion, quartered and thinly sliced
Thinly sliced lemons
Finely chopped fresh parsley

Rinse and sort the beans, discarding withered ones and checking carefully for small stones. Soak overnight in plenty of water, or cover with water, bring to a boil, then let stand off the heat for an hour.

Drain the beans and rinse. Place in a large soup pot with fresh water in a ratio of approximately 3 parts water to 1 part beans. Bring to a boil, then cover and simmer over low heat for 1 hour. Add the oil, chopped onion, carrots, celery, garlic, parsley, bay leaves, seasoning mix, nutmeg, and wine or sherry. Simmer for another 1 to 1½ hours, or until the beans are soft.

With a slotted spoon, scoop out about 1½ cups of the beans, avoiding as much as possible scooping out the other vegetables. Set aside.

Discard the bay leaves and transfer the solid ingredients, in batches, to the container of a food processor. Use about ¼ cup cooking liquid per batch. Process until smoothly puréed, then return the purée to the soup pot along with the reserved beans. Season to taste with salt and pepper and return to low heat for 15 minutes.

Just before serving, heat the margarine in a small skillet. Add the sliced onion and sauté over moderate heat until golden brown.

Garnish each serving with some of the sauteed onion, 2 lemon slices and some chopped parsley. This soup keeps very well for several days, and the flavor improves as it stands.

HOT-AND-SOUR ORIENTAL VEGETABLE SOUP

6 servings

Don't be intimidated by the long list of ingredients here. It's an easy soup to make, doesn't take long to cook, and is full of exciting textures and flavors.

6 dried shiitake mushrooms
1 tablespoon peanut oil
1 teaspoon dark sesame oil
1 medium onion, quartered and sliced
2 or 3 stalks bok choy or 2 large celery stalks
14-ounce can plum tomatoes
   with liquid, chopped
1 cup fresh mushrooms, coarsely chopped
5 cups water (include liquid from the canned baby
   corn and water chestnuts)
1 teaspoon lemon-pepper
1 cup snow peas, cut into 1-inch pieces
6-ounce can water chestnuts, sliced
16-ounce can baby corn
3 to 5 tablespoons rice vinegar, to taste
Chili oil, cayenne pepper, or any hot sauce
   (such as Tabasco), to taste
2 tablespoons natural soy sauce
½ pound firm tofu, cut into ½-inch dice
2 scallions, minced
2 tablespoons cornstarch

Place the dried mushrooms in a bowl to soak in about 1 cup of hot water. Set aside.

Heat the oils in a large soup pot. Add the onion and sauté over low heat until it is golden. Add the bok choy or celery, tomatoes, fresh mushrooms, water, and lemon-pepper. Bring to a boil, simmer over low heat, covered, until the bok choy or celery is tender-crisp, about 10 minutes.

In the meantime, trim and discard the tough stems of the soaked dried mushrooms. Slice the caps. Add them with their soaking liquid to the soup, along with the remaining ingredients, except the cornstarch. Taste frequently as you add the vinegar and hot seasoning. Simmer over very low heat for 8 to 10 minutes.

Dissolve the cornstarch in ¼ cup water. Slowly drizzle into the soup while stirring. Simmer over very low heat for another 5 minutes. Remove from the heat and serve at once.

SAUERKRAUT SOUP

6 to 8 servings

An offbeat, pungent-and-sweet soup that takes the chill out of a nippy fall afternoon. Serve with Onion-Rye Oven Scones (page 116), or a fresh, purchased rye bread.

1 tablespoon safflower oil
1 large onion, quartered and thinly sliced
2 medium carrots, thinly sliced
1 large celery stalk, finely diced
6 cups water
2 medium apples, peeled and finely diced
l-pound can sauerkraut, drained
14-ounce can plum tomatoes with liquid, chopped
1 teaspoon salt-free herb-and-spice seasoning mix
¼ cup light brown sugar, more or less to taste
2 cups cooked navy beans
Freshly ground pepper to taste

Heat the oil in a large soup pot. Add the onion and sauté until golden. Add the carrots, celery, and water. Bring to a boil, then cover and simmer over moderate heat for 15 minutes.

Add the remaining ingredients and simmer for another 30 to 40 minutes, or until the carrots and celery are tender. Add more water if the soup seems crowded, and adjust the seasonings. If time allows, let the soup stand off the heat for an hour or so before serving, then heat through as needed.

W·I·N·T·E·R

Winter is the very best time for soup—nothing offers better comfort when coming in from the cold. Despite the dearth of lively fresh produce, there are the homely root vegetables to work with, and it is a perfect time to make thick soups of grains and legumes. Teamed with bread and salad, most of the soups in this section make satisfying meals in and of themselves.

MINESTRONE

8 or more servings

Filling and flavorful, this Italian vegetable soup becomes a meal in itself when served with a robust bread such as Focaccia Bread (page 109). It keeps exceptionally well and develops flavor as it stands.

2 tablespoons olive oil
2 medium onions, finely chopped
2 cloves garlic, minced
2 medium carrots, diced
2 medium celery stalks, diced
Handful of celery leaves, chopped
2 medium potatoes, peeled and diced
2 cups shredded white cabbage
14-ounce can plum tomatoes with liquid, chopped
1 cup tomato sauce
¼ cup dry wine, optional
2 bay leaves
2 teaspoons Italian herb seasoning mix
2 cups cooked or canned chick-peas
1 cup frozen green peas, thawed
2 tablespoons minced fresh parsley
Salt and freshly ground pepper to taste

Heat the oil in a large soup pot. Add the onions and garlic and sauté over moderate heat until the onions are golden. Add the carrots, celery, celery leaves, potatoes, and cabbage, along with just enough water to cover. Add the tomatoes, tomato sauce, optional wine, bay leaves, and seasoning mix. Bring to just under the boiling point, then lower the heat and cook slowly over low heat, covered, until the vegetables are just done, about 45 minutes. Add the chick-peas, green peas, and parsley. Correct the consistency with more water if necessary, then season to taste with salt and pepper. Simmer over low heat for at least another 20 to 30 minutes, or until the vegetables are completely tender, but not overdone.

The making of a good soup is quite an art, and many otherwise clever cooks do not possess the tour de main necessary to its successful preparation. Either they over-complicate the composition of the dish, or they attach only minor importance to it, reserving their talents for the meal itself, and so it frequently happens that the soup does not correspond to the quality of the rest of the dishes; nevertheless, the quality of the soup should foretell that of the entire meal.

—Madame Seignobos
  Comment on forme une cuisiniere, 1903

ITALIAN PASTA AND BEAN SOUP

8 or more servings

Like Minestrone, this is an Italian standard. Serve it with Parmesan Pita wedges (page 120).

2 tablespoons extra-virgin olive oil
1 medium onion, finely chopped
2 cloves garlic, minced
1 medium carrot, cut into ¼-inch dice
7 cups cooking liquid from beans or water
3 cups cooked or canned Great Northern beans
2 cups diced zucchini
2 bay leaves
1½ teaspoons Italian herb seasoning mix
¼ cup tomato paste
1½ cups tiny, tubular pasta
2 tablespoons chopped fresh parsley
Salt and freshly ground pepper to taste

Heat the olive oil in a large soup pot. Add the onion, garlic, and carrot, and sauté over moderate heat, stirring frequently, until the onion is golden. Add the water, beans, zucchini, bay leaves, seasoning mix, and tomato paste. Bring to a boil, then cover and simmer over low heat until the zucchini is just tender, about 10 minutes. Remove from the heat and allow the soup to stand for an hour or so to develop flavor.

In a separate saucepan, cook the pasta *al dente*. Rinse briefly under cool water until it stops steaming. Add the parsley to the soup and heat it through. When hot, add the cooked pasta, and season to taste with salt and pepper. Serve at once.

MACARONI AND CHEESE SOUP

6 to 8 servings

A smooth, mild soup, this melds puréed white beans with cheese and pasta for a high-protein result.

2 tablespoons margarine
1 large onion, finely chopped
2 medium celery stalks, finely diced
2 cups well-cooked or canned navy or
  Great Northern beans
3½ cups Light Vegetable Stock (page 10) or water
½ pound mushrooms, coarsely chopped
1½ teaspoons salt-free herb-and-spice seasoning mix
1 cup low-fat milk or soymilk, or as needed
1½ cups firmly packed grated Cheddar cheese
  or Cheddar-style soy cheese
2 cups small pasta, such as shells or elbows
Salt to taste
Dash cayenne pepper

Heat the margarine in a large soup pot. Add the onion and celery and sauté over moderately low heat until the onion is golden.

In the meantime, purée the beans in a blender or food processor until smooth.

Cover the onion and celery with the water or stock. Bring to a boil, then stir in the bean purée, mushrooms, and seasoning mix. Simmer for 30 to 35 minutes. Stir in the milk or soy milk, more or less as needed to achieve a slightly thick consistency. Remove from the heat and sprinkle in the cheese, a bit at a time, stirring in each time until it disappears. Cover the soup and set aside.

In a separate saucepan, cook the pasta *al dente*. Drain it and stir into the soup. Adjust the consistency of the soup with more milk or soymilk, if needed, then return to low heat. Season to taste with salt and cayenne. Remove the soup from the heat once it is thoroughly heated through and serve.

WINTER CELERY, POTATO, AND MUSHROOM SOUP

6 servings

This is just the sort of mild soup that is so comforting on cold winter days. Quick Sunflower-Cheese Bread (page 108) is a good accompaniment, as are Cheddar-Oat Griddle Biscuits (page 114).

2 tablespoons safflower oil
1 large or 2 medium onions, chopped
2 tablespoons unbleached white flour
5 cups Light Vegetable Stock (page 10) or water
4 large celery stalks, diced
Handful of celery leaves
3 medium potatoes, diced
⅓ cup raw pearl or pot barley, rinsed
2 bay leaves
½ pound coarsely chopped mushrooms
2 teaspoons salt-free herb-and-spice seasoning mix
1 cup frozen green peas, thawed
1½ to 2 cups low-fat milk or soymilk, or as needed
Salt and freshly ground pepper to taste

Heat the safflower oil in a large soup pot. Add the onion and sauté until golden. Sprinkle in the flour, a bit at a time, and stir in until it disappears. Slowly pour in the water or stock, then add the celery, celery leaves, potatoes, barley, and bay leaves. Bring to a boil, then cover and simmer over low heat for 15 minutes. Next add the mushrooms and seasoning mix and simmer until the barley is tender, another 20 to 30 minutes.

Add the green peas and enough milk or soymilk to achieve a medium-thick consistency. Season to taste with salt and pepper and simmer over very low heat for another 10 minutes.

This soup thickens as it stands; thin any leftovers with additional milk or soymilk, then taste to correct the seasonings.

Eat soup first and eat it last,
and live till a hundred years be past.

—French proverb

CREAMY PARSNIP-VEGETABLE SOUP

6 servings

This soothing winter soup is much more elegant than its name implies. To make it even more homey and filling, serve it with any of the dumplings on pages 122 to 124.

2 tablespoons margarine
1½ cups chopped onion
1 large celery stalk, diced
Handful of celery leaves
1 pound parsnips, scraped and cut into ½-inch dice
2 large potatoes, peeled and cut into ½-inch dice
2 medium carrots, coarsely chopped
14-ounce can plum tomatoes with liquid, chopped
1½ teaspoons salt-free herb-and-spice seasoning mix
2 tablespoons minced fresh parsley
1½ to 2 cups whole milk or soymilk, as needed
Salt and freshly ground pepper to taste

Heat the margarine in a large soup pot. Add the onion and celery and sauté until the onion is golden. Add the celery leaves, parsnips, potatoes, carrots, tomatoes, seasoning mix, and just enough water to cover. Bring to a boil, then simmer over moderately low heat, covered, until the vegetables are tender, about 20 to 30 minutes. Remove from the heat.

With a slotted spoon, transfer half of the vegetables to the container of a food processor or blender. Process until smoothly puréed, then stir back into the soup. Stir in the parsley and enough milk or soymilk to achieve a slightly thick consistency. Season to taste with salt and pepper. Return the soup to very low heat for 10 to 15 minutes; do not let it boil. This soup thickens as it cools. Adjust the consistency of any leftover soup with additional water, milk, or soymilk, and taste to correct the seasonings.

HEARTY WINTER ROOTS SOUP

6 to 8 servings

When I first devised this soup of homely winter root vegetables, the result was much more elegant than I expected. Any of the dumplings on pages 122 to 124 will add a nice touch.

2 tablespoons margarine
1 large onion, chopped
2 cups peeled, diced rutabaga
2 medium carrots, coarsely chopped
2 medium potatoes, scrubbed and diced
2 medium parsnips, diced
1 large celery stalk, diced
⅓ cup rolled oats, rolled wheat, or rolled rye
¼ cup dry white wine
2 teaspoons salt-free herb-and-spice seasoning mix
1½ cups low-fat milk or soymilk, or as needed
1 cup grated Cheddar cheese
   or Cheddar-style soy cheese
Salt and freshly ground pepper to taste

Heat the margarine in a large soup pot. Add the onion and sauté over moderate heat until it is golden. Add the vegetables along with just enough water to cover. Add all the remaining ingredients except the last 3, and stir together well. Bring to a boil, then simmer over low heat, covered, until the vegetables are tender, about 30 to 40 minutes. With a slotted spoon, remove about 2 cups of the vegetables and mash coarsely, then stir back into the soup. Add the milk or soymilk and allow the soup to simmer over very low heat for another 10 minutes.

Sprinkle in the cheese, a little at a time, stirring it in until it disappears each time. If the soup is too thick, adjust the consistency with a bit more milk or soymilk, then season to taste with salt and pepper. If time allows, let the soup stand for an hour or so before serving, then heat through slowly, over low heat, as needed.

GOLDEN CURRIED PEA SOUP

6 to 8 Servings

The complementary protein of the peas and rice make this easy winter soup a natural choice as a hearty main dish. Make Whole Wheat Vegetable Muffins (page 110) to go along with it, plus a simple, palate-cooling salad of cucumbers dressed in yogurt.

2 tablespoons margarine
1 cup finely chopped onion
1 large potato, diced
2 to 3 cloves garlic, crushed or minced
8 cups Light Vegetable Stock (page 10) or water
1 pound dried yellow split peas, rinsed
½ cup raw brown rice, rinsed
2 bay leaves
2 teaspoons good-quality curry powder or *garam masala*,
**   more or less to taste**
1 teaspoon freshly grated ginger
Salt to taste

Heat the margarine in a large soup pot. Add the onion and sauté over moderately low heat until it is golden. Add all the remaining ingredients except the salt. Bring to a boil, then simmer over low heat, covered, until the peas are mushy, about 1½ hours. Stir occasionally. When the peas are done, adjust the consistency with more water or stock as needed, then season to taste with salt. This soup thickens considerably as it stands; thin with additional water or stock and adjust the seasonings.

CURRIED MILLET-SPINACH SOUP

8 servings

Millet, an exceptionally nutritious but rather bland grain, is used to great advantage in this soup, where it has an opportunity to soak up all the spicy flavors.

8 cups water
2 tablespoons margarine
¾ cup millet, rinsed in a fine sieve
1 cup chopped onion
2 cloves garlic, minced
2 medium potatoes, diced
1 large carrot, coarsely chopped
14-ounce can plum tomatoes with liquid, chopped
1 teaspoon freshly grated ginger
2 teaspoons good-quality curry powder or *garam masala,*
    more or less to taste
10-ounce package frozen chopped spinach, thawed
2 tablespoons finely chopped fresh parsley
Juice of ½ lemon
Salt and freshly ground pepper to taste

Combine all the ingredients except the last 4 in a large soup pot. Bring to a boil, then simmer over moderate heat, covered, for 1 to 1½ hours, or until the millet and vegetables are tender. Stir in the spinach, parsley, and lemon juice. If the soup is too thick, add a bit more water. Season to taste with salt and pepper and simmer over very low heat for another 10 to 15 minutes.

This soup thickens as it stands, especially after refrigeration. Adjust the consistency with water, then correct the seasonings.

SPICY CHILI BEAN SOUP

8 or more servings

For those who like "hot stuff," the hot chilies add a fiery kick to this soup. If you'd like a more toned-down version, use mild chilies.

1 pound dry kidney, red, or pink beans
1 large onion, chopped
2 to 3 cloves garlic, minced
2 bay leaves
2 tablespoons olive oil, divided
14-ounce can plum tomatoes with liquid, chopped
¾ cup tomato sauce
⅓ cup raw brown rice, rinsed
2 teaspoons chili powder, more or less to taste
2 fresh hot green chilies, seeded and chopped
1 cup fresh cooked or frozen corn kernels
Salt to taste
1 large green bell pepper, cut into l-inch strips
Grated Cheddar cheese or Cheddar-style
** soy cheese for topping**

Soak the beans overnight in plenty of water. Once you're ready to begin the soup, drain them and cover them with fresh water in a ratio of about double the water to the volume of beans. Add the onion and garlic, bring to a boil, then cover and simmer over low heat for 1 to 1½ hours, or until the beans are tender (press one between your thumb and forefinger—if it yields easily, this is the right texture).

Add the bay leaves, half of the oil, the tomatoes, tomato sauce, rice, chili powder, and chopped chilies. Return to a boil, then cover and simmer over low heat until the rice is done, about 45 minutes, or a bit longer. Stir in the corn kernels and season with salt. Continue to simmer over very low heat.

Heat the remaining olive oil in a small skillet. Add the green bell pepper and sauté, stirring frequently, until it is fragrant and just lightly touched with brown. Remove from the heat.

Top each serving of soup with a few strips of sautéed bell peppers, and a small quantity of grated cheese.

Beans possess over all vegetables the great advantage of being just as good, if not better, when kept waiting, an advantage in the case of people whose disposition or occupation makes it difficult for them to be punctual.

—Andre Simon
   The Concise Dictionary of Gastronomy, 1952

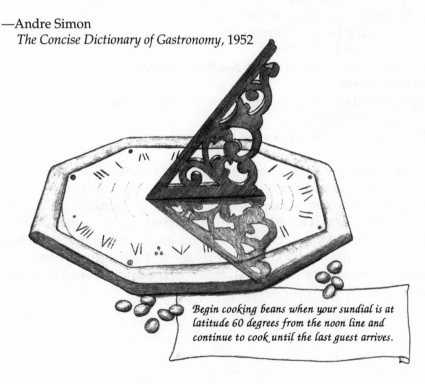

Begin cooking beans when your sundial is at latitude 60 degrees from the noon line and continue to cook until the last guest arrives.

BROWN RICE AND THREE BEAN SOUP

8 servings

2 tablespoons olive oil
1 large onion, chopped
6 cups cooking liquid from beans or water
1 large celery stalk, diced
½ cup raw brown rice, rinsed
14-ounce can plum tomatoes with liquid, chopped
1½ teaspoons Italian herb seasoning mix
1 teaspoon chili powder
1 tablespoon natural soy sauce
½ pound string beans, trimmed and
    cut into ½- to l-inch pieces
2 cups cooked or canned Great Northern beans
    or navy beans
2 cups cooked or canned kidney, red, or pink beans
1 tablespoon lemon juice
Salt and freshly ground pepper to taste

Heat the oil in a large soup pot. Add the onion and sauté over moderate heat until it is golden. Add the water or the cooking liquid from beans, along with the celery, rice, tomatoes, seasonings, and soy sauce. Bring to a boil, then cover and simmer over low heat for 30 minutes. Add the string beans and the two other types of beans. Simmer for another 30 to 45 minutes, or until the rice and beans are quite tender. Stir in the lemon juice, then season to taste with salt and pepper. If time allows, let the soup stand for an hour or longer before serving, then heat through as needed.

Next to the Emperor, rice is the most sacred of all things on earth.

—*Japanese proverb*

HEARTY BARLEY-BEAN SOUP

6 to 8 servings

This is a good, basic "everyday" sort of soup, suitable for cold weather. Try Cheese and Herb Corn Muffins (page 111) with it.

2 tablespoons olive oil
2 large onions, chopped
2 cloves garlic, minced
¾ cup raw pearl or pot barley, rinsed
2 large celery stalks, diced
Handful of celery greens
1 bay leaf
2½ teaspoons salt-free herb-and-spice seasoning mix
14-ounce can plum tomatoes with liquid, chopped
6 cups water or cooking liquid from beans
2 heaping cups cooked or canned kidney,
    red, or pink beans
3 tablespoons chopped fresh parsley
2 tablespoons minced fresh dill
Salt and freshly ground pepper to taste

Heat the oil in a large soup pot. Add the onions and garlic and sauté over moderate heat until the onions are golden. Add all the remaining ingredients except the last 4. Bring to a boil, then simmer over low heat, covered, for 1 hour. At this time the barley and vegetables should be tender. Add the beans, parsley, and dill. Season to taste with salt and pepper, then simmer for another 30 minutes over low heat.

You may serve this at once, or allow the soup to stand for an hour or so before serving, then heat through as needed. As the soup stands, it will thicken; adjust the consistency as needed with additional water, then correct the seasonings.

CREAMY MUNG BEAN SOUP

8 servings

Mung beans—small, olive-colored legumes—are well-loved in Indian cuisine. Serve with Barley or Rice Triangles (page 113) or Oat-Chive Dumplings (page 123).

2 tablespoons margarine
2 large onions, chopped
5 to 6 cloves garlic, minced
1 pound mung beans, rinsed
2 medium carrots, coarsely chopped
1 teaspoon freshly grated ginger, more or less to taste
1½ teaspoons good-quality curry powder
   or *garam masala*, more or less to taste
¼ cup chopped fresh cilantro or parsley
2 cups low-fat milk or soymilk, or as needed
Salt and freshly ground pepper to taste

Heat the margarine in a large soup pot. Add the onion and sauté over moderate heat until it is translucent. Add the garlic and continue to sauté until the onion is golden and just beginning to be touched with brown. Add the mung beans along with 10 cups of water. Bring to a boil, then simmer, covered, over low heat for 30 minutes. Add the carrots, ginger, and curry powder. Simmer for another 1 to 1 ½ hours, or until the mung beans are tender and slightly mushy. Remove from the heat.

With a slotted spoon, transfer half of the solid ingredients to the container of a food processor or blender, along with about ½ cup of the liquid. Process until smoothly puréed, then stir back into the soup pot. Stir in the cilantro or parsley, followed by enough milk or soymilk to give the soup a slightly thick consistency. Season to taste with salt and pepper. Simmer over very low heat for 15 minutes, then serve.

CURRIED LENTIL, POTATO, AND CAULIFLOWER SOUP

6 to 8 servings

Lentil soups are so satisfying in the winter. Served with Quick Sunflower-Cheese Bread (page 108) or Focaccia Bread (page 109), you'll need only a simple salad to make a very filling meal.

2 tablespoons margarine
1 large onion, chopped
1 cup lentils, rinsed
1 large celery stalk, diced
3 to 4 cloves garlic, minced
2 bay leaves
2 large potatoes, scrubbed and diced
14-ounce can plum tomatoes with liquid, chopped
2 teaspoons good-quality curry powder or *garam masala,*
     more or less to taste
2½ cups finely chopped cauliflower pieces
1 cup finely chopped fresh spinach leaves
2 tablespoons chopped fresh cilantro, if available
Juice of ½ lemon
Salt and freshly ground pepper to taste

Heat the margarine in a large soup pot. Add the onion and sauté over moderately low heat until it is golden. Add 7 cups water, lentils, celery, garlic, and bay leaves. Bring to a boil, then simmer, covered, over moderately low heat, about 10 minutes. Add the potatoes, tomatoes, and curry powder, and simmer until the potatoes are half done, about 10 to 15 minutes. Add the cauliflower and simmer until the lentils and vegetables are tender, another 20 minutes or so. Stir in the spinach, cilantro, and lemon juice. Correct the consistency with more water if necessary, then season to taste with salt and pepper. Simmer over very low heat for another 5 minutes. Serve at once or let stand for an hour before serving, then heat through as needed.

The philosophers Virgil and Pliny credited lentils with the ability to produce temperaments of mildness and moderation in those who consumed them.

To improve the temperament of a surly husband, feed him lentils daily.

TOMATO, LENTIL, AND BARLEY SOUP

6 to 8 servings

½ pound dry lentils, rinsed
¾ cup raw pearl or pot barley, rinsed
6 cups water
1 tablespoon olive oil
1 large onion, chopped
1 clove garlic, minced
2 large celery stalks, diced
2 medium carrots, sliced
1 cup white cabbage, shredded
28-ounce can plum tomatoes with liquid, chopped
¼ cup dry red wine
1 tablespoon apple-cider vinegar
¼ cup chopped fresh parsley
2 teaspoons salt-free herb-and-spice seasoning mix
Salt and freshly ground pepper to taste

Combine the lentils and barley in a large soup pot with the water and bring to a boil. Add all the remaining ingredients except the salt and pepper, return to a boil, then simmer slowly over low heat, covered, until everything is tender, about 45 to 55 minutes. Stir occasionally and add more water if the soup becomes too thick. Season to taste with salt and pepper. If time allows, let the soup stand for an hour or so before serving, then heat through as needed.

TOMATO, CHICK-PEA, AND BULGUR SOUP

6 to 8 servings

Bulgur (presteamed, cracked wheat, commonly available in natural food stores) is rarely used in soups, but works very nicely, adding protein and a chewy texture.

2½ tablespoons olive oil, divided
1 large onion, chopped
2 to 3 cloves garlic, minced
2 large celery stalks, diced
2 medium white turnips, diced
½ cup finely shredded cabbage
½ cup raw bulgur
28-ounce can plum tomatoes with liquid, chopped
5 cups water or cooking liquid from chick-peas
2 bay leaves
2 teaspoons Italian herb seasoning mix
1 teaspoon paprika
2 to 2½ cups well-cooked or canned chick-peas
Salt and freshly ground pepper to taste
1 medium green bell pepper, cut into thin,
    l-inch-long strips

Heat 1½ tablespoons of the oil in a large soup pot. Add the onion and sauté over moderate heat until it is golden. Add all the remaining ingredients except for the last 3, bring to a boil, then cover and simmer over low heat until the bulgur and all the vegetables are tender, about 35 to 40 minutes. Add the chick-peas, then season to taste with salt and pepper. Simmer for another 15 minutes. If time allows, let the soup stand for about an hour before serving, then heat through as needed.

Just before serving, heat the remaining tablespoon of olive oil in a small skillet. Sauté the bell pepper until it is just lightly touched with brown spots. After ladling the soup into bowls, top each serving with some of the sautéed pepper.

MISO SOUP WITH WINTER VEGETABLES

6 servings

This winter miso soup is very warming. See page 12 for further information on miso, under Simple Miso Broth.

6-inch piece wakame (Japanese sea vegetable), optional
2 tablespoons safflower or peanut oil
2 medium onions, quartered and sliced
4 medium potatoes, peeled and finely diced
1½ cups shredded savoy or white cabbage
1 large celery stalk, cut in matchstick-shaped pieces
1 large carrot, cut in matchstick-shaped pieces
1 recipe Oriental Mushroom Broth (page 14)
Sliced shiitake mushrooms from above broth
¼ cup dry red wine or sherry
1 teaspoon freshly grated ginger
½ teaspoon lemon-pepper
2 to 3 tablespoons miso, to taste

If you'd like to use the wakame, wipe the piece with a damp sponge, then soak it in lukewarm water for 10 minutes. Drain and chop the wakame and set aside.

Heat the oil in a large soup pot. Add the onions and sauté until golden. Add the potatoes, cabbage, celery, carrot, and the Oriental Mushroom Broth. Trim the mushrooms used in making the broth of their tough stems, then slice the caps and add them to the soup along with the chopped wakame, red wine or sherry, ginger, and lemon-pepper. Bring to a boil, then simmer over low heat for 25 to 30 minutes, or until the vegetables are done, but still have a bit of firmness.

Dissolve the miso in just enough water to make it smooth and pourable. Stir it into the soup, then remove from the heat and serve.

S·P·R·I·N·G

After the thick, hearty soups of winter, those presented here offer the palate a lift with lighter textures and flavors. Whereas many of the winter soups could function as main dishes, these spring soups set the stage for a meal—they'll take the edge off of hunger, but leave room for other courses.

PURÉE OF ASPARAGUS
WITH BUCKWHEAT NOODLES

6 servings

Nutty-tasting, dark buckwheat noodles, traditional to Japan, add an unusual element to this soup. Look for them in natural food stores or Oriental groceries.

2 pounds asparagus
1 tablespoon dark sesame oil or unrefined
  peanut oil
1 large onion, chopped
2 large celery stalks, diced
2 medium potatoes, scrubbed and diced
4½ cups Light Vegetable Stock (page 10) or water
1½ teaspoons salt-free herb-and-spice seasoning mix
2 tablespoons natural soy sauce
¼ pound buckwheat noodles
Freshly ground pepper to taste
Slivered or chopped almonds for garnish
Minced chives or scallions for garnish

Trim the tough ends off of the asparagus, and peel any tough skin with a vegetable peeler. Cut the asparagus into 1-inch lengths. Reserve and set aside the tips.

Heat the oil in a large soup pot. Add the onion and sauté until golden. Add the celery, potatoes, water or stock, seasoning mix, and soy sauce. Bring to a boil, then simmer over low heat, covered, for 10 minutes. Add the asparagus pieces (not the tips) and simmer for another 15 minutes, or until the vegetables are tender. Remove from the heat.

With a slotted spoon, transfer the solid ingredients to the container of a food processor or blender. Purée in batches until smooth and stir back into the liquid in the soup pot. Return to very low heat. Correct the consistency if necessary with additional water or stock, then taste to correct the seasonings.

Break the buckwheat noodles into 1- to 2-inch lengths. In a separate saucepan, cook them in rapidly simmering water until they are *al dente*. Drain and rinse them briefly under cool water. At the same time, steam the reserved asparagus tips until they are bright green. Stir both the noodles and asparagus tips into the soup. Add freshly ground pepper to taste and remove from the heat.

Serve at once, garnishing each serving with the almonds and chives or scallions.

Asparagus is a delicate fruit, and wholesome for everiebodie, and especially when it is thicke, tender and sweet...it maketh a good color in the face.

—Anonymous
  Maison Rustique, 1600

LEEK AND MUSHROOM BISQUE

6 to 8 servings

Farina is the secret to the smooth, thick texture of this soup.

3 large leeks
2 tablespoons margarine
5 cups water
14- or 16-ounce can puréed tomatoes
½ cup farina (cream of wheat)
12 ounces mushrooms, coarsely chopped or sliced
2 teaspoons salt-free herb-and-spice seasoning mix
1½ to 2 cups low-fat milk or soymilk, as needed
Salt and freshly ground pepper to taste

Slice the white part of the leeks into ¼-inch slices. Separate the slices into rings, then rinse well to remove all grit. Wash the green parts of the leeks well and cut them in half.

Heat the margarine in a large soup pot. Add the white parts of the leeks and sauté over moderate heat until they are limp. Add the water and tomato purée, bring to a boil, then lower the heat until the water is at a gentle, steady simmer. Slowly sprinkle in the farina, stirring it in as you do. Add the green parts of the leeks, the mushrooms, and the seasoning mix. Cover and simmer over low heat for 35 minutes. Remove the green parts of the leeks and discard.

Stir in enough milk or soymilk to give a slightly thick consistency, then season to taste with salt and pepper. Simmer for another 5 minutes. Remove from the heat and let the soup stand for at least an hour before serving. Heat through as needed, then adjust the consistency with more milk if necessary, and correct the seasonings.

CURRIED CAULIFLOWER-CHEESE SOUP

6 to 8 servings

2 tablespoons margarine
1 large onion, chopped
2 medium celery stalks, diced
3 medium potatoes, peeled and cut into ½-inch dice
1 medium head cauliflower, finely chopped
Light Vegetable Stock (page 10) or water
2 teaspoons good-quality curry powder or *garam masala,*
   more or less to taste
1 cup low-fat milk or soymilk, or as needed
1 cup steamed fresh green peas,
   or thawed frozen green peas
3 tablespoons minced fresh dill,
   or 1 tablespoon dried dill
1½ cups firmly packed grated mild white cheese,
   or Mozzarella-style soy cheese
Salt and freshly ground pepper to taste

Heat the margarine in a large soup pot. Add the onion and celery, and sauté over moderately low heat until the onion is golden. Add the potatoes, cauliflower, and enough water or stock to barely cover. Stir in the curry powder. Bring to a boil, then cover and simmer until all the vegetables are tender, about 20 to 25 minutes. Remove from the heat.

With a slotted spoon, transfer half of the solid ingredients to the container of a food processor or blender. Process until smoothly puréed. Stir back into the remaining soup. Add just enough milk or soymilk to achieve a slightly thick consistency. Stir in the peas and dill. Return to low heat and bring to a gentle simmer. Sprinkle the cheese in a bit at a time, stirring in until thoroughly melted each time.

Adjust the consistency with more milk if necessary, then season to taste with salt and pepper. Serve once the soup is thoroughly heated through.

CURRIED CASHEW SOUP

6 servings

Cashews make an unusual and rich-tasting base for a soup. This delicious soup is good hot or at room temperature.

1½ tablespoons safflower or unrefined peanut oil
2 large onions, chopped
3 to 4 cloves garlic, minced
1 large celery stalk, diced
1½ cups toasted cashew pieces
1 teaspoon minced fresh ginger
2 teaspoons good quality curry powder or *garam masala,*
  more or less to taste
1 tablespoon lemon juice
Juice of 1 fresh orange
3 cups steamed fresh green vegetables (such as
  finely chopped broccoli, green peas, diced zucchini,
  or any combination)
Salt to taste
Chopped cashews for garnish

Heat the oil in a skillet. Add the onions, garlic, and celery and sauté over moderate heat until all are lightly browned. Remove from the heat. Place the cashews in the container of a food processor or blender. Process until they resemble a very fine meal, then add the onion mixture from the skillet, the ginger, and 1 cup of water. Process until well puréed.

Transfer the mixture into a large soup pot along with 4 cups more water, the curry powder, and lemon and orange juices. Bring to a boil, then simmer over low heat for 30 minutes. Remove from the heat and let stand for 30 minutes to 1 hour.

Return to moderate heat. Add the steamed vegetables and adjust if necessary with more water to achieve a slightly thick consistency. Season to taste with salt, then serve once the soup is heated through. Garnish each serving with a few chopped cashews.

Augustus was a chubby lad,
Fat ruddy cheeks Augustus had,
And everybody saw with joy,
The plump and hearty, healthy boy.
He ate and drank as he was told,
And never let his soup get cold.

—Heinrich Hoffman (1809-74)

CREOLE EGGPLANT SOUP

6 servings

Courtesy of the famous Commander's Palace restaurant in New Orleans, this soup was a favorite discovery while on a journey across the American south.

2 tablespoons margarine
1 large onion, chopped
3 medium celery stalks, diced
1 clove garlic, minced
1½ tablespoons unbleached white flour
2 large potatoes, peeled and finely diced
1 large or 2 medium eggplants (1½ pounds total),
   peeled and finely diced
1 teaspoon dried basil
¼ teaspoon dried thyme
1 teaspoon good-quality curry powder or *garam masala*
2 to 3 tablespoons chopped fresh parsley
1 cup low-fat milk or soymilk, or as needed
Salt and freshly ground pepper to taste

Heat the margarine in a large soup pot. Add the onion, celery, and garlic and sauté over low heat, stirring frequently, for 10 minutes. Add a small amount of water if the mixture becomes dry. Sprinkle in the flour and cook, stirring, for another minute. Place the potato and diced eggplant in the soup pot along with enough water to cover all but about an inch of the vegetables. Bring to a boil. At this point you should be able to push all the vegetables below the water line. Add the seasonings and stir well. Cover and simmer over low heat for 40 minutes, or until the vegetables are quite tender.

Stir in the parsley and enough milk to achieve a slightly thick consistency. Season to taste with salt and pepper. Simmer over very low heat for another 5 to 10 minutes and serve, or let the soup stand off the heat for an hour or so, then heat through as needed.

MEDITERRANEAN EGGPLANT SOUP

6 to 8 servings

A colorful medley of Italian flavors, this soup is a perfect introduction to a light meal—perhaps an omelet, a salad of crisp greens, and a good white wine. Try Parmesan Pita Wedges (page 120) as an accompaniment.

2 tablespoons olive oil
1 large onion, chopped
2 cloves garlic, pressed or minced
2 large celery stalks, finely diced
2 medium eggplants (about 1½ pounds in all),
    peeled and cut into ½-inch dice
28-ounce can plum tomatoes with liquid, chopped
2 teaspoons Italian herb seasoning mix
1 cup raw pasta, any small shape such as shells or twists
¼ cup finely chopped fresh parsley
Salt and freshly ground pepper to taste

Heat the oil in a large soup pot. Add the onion, garlic, and celery and sauté over moderate heat until the onion is golden. Add 5 cups of water, the diced eggplant, the tomatoes, and the seasoning mix. Bring to a boil, then simmer over low heat, covered, until the eggplant is tender, about 45 minutes.

In the meantime, cook the pasta separately until it is done *al dente*. Drain and stir into the soup along with the parsley. Adjust the consistency with more water if the soup has gotten too thick. Season to taste with salt and pepper. Simmer over very low heat another 15 minutes. This soup may be served at once, but if you have time to let it stand for an hour or more, so much the better. Heat through as needed before serving.

WHITE BEAN PURÉE WITH ZUCCHINI AND HERBS

6 to 8 servings

Any of the dumplings on pages 122 to 124 add a nice touch to this soup, or serve it with any of the muffins on pages 110 to 112.

2 tablespoons margarine, divided
1 large onion, chopped
1 clove garlic, minced
4 cups well-cooked or canned Great Northern beans
4 cups cooking liquid from beans, water,
   or Light Vegetable Stock (page 10)
¼ cup dry white wine
3 tablespoons each: chopped fresh parsley
   and minced fresh dill
1 teaspoon good-quality curry powder or *garam masala*
1 medium zucchini
Juice of ½ to 1 lemon, to taste
Salt and freshly ground pepper to taste

Heat half of the margarine in a skillet. Add the onion and sauté over moderate heat until it is translucent. Add the garlic and continue to sauté until the mixture is lightly browned. Transfer the mixture to the container of a food processor or blender along with about half of the beans. Process until smoothly puréed. Put the purée in a large soup pot along with the remaining beans, the liquid, wine, parsley, dill, and curry powder. Bring to a gentle simmer, then continue to simmer over very low heat, covered, for 20 minutes.

In the meantime, cut the zucchini lengthwise into quarters, then into ¼-inch-thick slices. Heat the remaining margarine in the skillet. Add the zucchini and a tablespoon of water and sauté over moderate heat, stirring frequently, until some of the pieces are lightly touched with brown. Stir into the soup. Adjust the consistency with more liquid if too thick. Season to taste with lemon juice, salt, and pepper and simmer for another 10 minutes over very low heat. If time allows, let the soup stand off the heat for at least an hour to allow flavor to develop, then heat through before serving.

If pale beans bubble for you in a red earthen-ware pot, you can often decline the dinners of sumptuous hosts.

—Martial (c. A.D. 40-104)
   Epigrams

TOMATO-RICE SOUP WITH SNOW PEAS

6 to 8 servings

Crisp green snow peas lend this soup a pleasant visual and textural twist.

2 tablespoons margarine
1 large onion, chopped
2 large celery stalks, diced
⅔ cup raw brown rice, rinsed
28-ounce can tomato purée
2 bay leaves
2 teaspoons Italian herb seasoning mix
1 heaping cup sliced mushrooms
3 to 4 tablespoons chopped fresh parsley
Salt and freshly ground pepper to taste
6 ounces snow peas, trimmed and cut into 1-inch pieces

Heat the margarine in a large soup pot. Add the onion and sauté over moderate heat until golden. Add 4 cups of water, followed by the celery, rice, tomato purée, bay leaves, and seasoning mix and bring to a boil. Simmer over low heat, covered, until the rice is just done, about 40 to 45 minutes. Add the mushrooms and parsley and correct the consistency with additional water if the soup is too thick. Simmer over low heat for another 15 minutes. Season to taste with salt and pepper. If time allows, let the soup stand for an hour or so before serving, then heat through as needed.

Before serving, steam the snow peas until bright green and tender-crisp. After ladling the soup into bowls, garnish each serving with some snow peas.

POTAGE MAIGRE

(Lettuce, Cucumber, and Fresh Pea Soup)

6 to 8 servings

This light soup of lettuce, cucumber, and fresh spring peas was quite common in 19th-century America. "Potage Maigre" translates loosely as a Fast-Day soup. Versions of it appear in old Creole and Pennsylvania Dutch cookbooks.

2 tablespoons margarine
2 large onions, quartered and thinly sliced
1 large celery stalk, finely diced
Handful of celery leaves
2 small heads Boston or Bibb lettuce, finely shredded
5 cups Light Vegetable Stock (page 10) or water
1 cup steamed fresh green peas
1 cup grated, peeled, and seeded cucumber
¼ cup chopped fresh parsley
2 tablespoons chopped fresh dill
Salt and freshly ground pepper to taste
Parsley-Potato Dumplings (page 122), optional,
    or sour cream or yogurt, optional

Heat the margarine in a large soup pot. Add the onions and sauté over moderately low heat until they are translucent. Add the diced celery and continue to sauté until the onions begin to turn golden. Add the celery leaves, lettuce, and stock or water. Bring to a boil, then cover and simmer for 10 to 15 minutes, or until the lettuce is wilted but still has a bit of crunch.

Add the peas, cucumber, and fresh herbs. Adjust the consistency with a bit more stock or water if the vegetables seem crowded. Season to taste with salt and lots of freshly ground pepper. Simmer over very low heat for another 10 minutes.

Serve hot with the optional Parsely-Potato Dumplings, or if you'd like, cool to room temperature and top each serving with a dollop of sour cream or yogurt.

OKRA-RICE GUMBO

6 to 8 servings

A classic from the American south, this thick concoction was as commonplace in the 19th century as it is unusual today. The result is a wonderfully diverse blend of flavors and textures—thanks mainly to the unique character of okra. Serve with fresh Buttermilk Oat Muffins (page 112).

2 tablespoons margarine
2 medium onions, chopped
2 medium celery stalks
14-ounce can plum tomatoes with liquid, chopped
4 cups young okra, sliced ½-inch thick
1 medium green bell pepper, chopped
⅔ cup raw brown rice, rinsed
2 bay leaves
1½ teaspoons salt-free herb-and-spice seasoning mix
¼ teaspoon dried red pepper flakes
   or cayenne pepper to taste
Salt and freshly ground pepper to taste

Heat the margarine in a large soup pot. Add the onions and celery and sauté over low heat until the onions just begin to turn golden. Add 5 cups of water and all the remaining ingredients except the salt and pepper. Enough red pepper flakes or cayenne should be used to give the soup a distinct bite, but use your discretion. Bring to a boil, then simmer over moderately low heat, covered, stirring occasionally, for about an hour, or until the rice is cooked and the vegetables are tender. Season to taste with salt and pepper.

Serve at once, or let the soup stand for an hour or so, then heat through as needed. The soup will thicken considerably as it stands. Adjust the consistency with more water as needed, and correct the seasonings, but let it remain very thick.

The great dish of New Orleans, and which it claims the honor of having invented, is the Gumbo. There is no dish which at the same time so tickles the palate, satisfies the appetite, furnishes the body with nutriment sufficient to carry on the physical requirements, and costs so little, as the Creole Gumbo. It is a dinner in itself, being soup, pièce de résistance and vegetable in one. Healthy, not heating to the stomach, and easy of digestion, it should grace every table.

—William Coleman, 1885

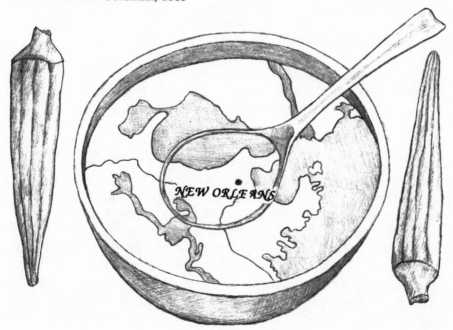

CREAM OF BROCCOLI SOUP
WITH WHOLE WHEAT PASTA

6 or more servings

2 large bunches broccoli
3 tablespoons margarine, divided
2 medium onions, chopped
2 cloves garlic, minced
1 large celery stalk, diced
2 tablespoons unbleached white flour
1 large tomato, chopped
¼ cup firmly packed chopped fresh parsley
2 teaspoons salt-free herb-and-spice seasoning mix
Light Vegetable Stock (page 10) or water
2 cups low-fat milk or soymilk, or as needed
1 cup small whole wheat shell or elbow pasta
Salt and freshly ground pepper to taste
Grated Parmesan cheese or Parmesan-style
    soy cheese for topping

Finely chop the broccoli, then set aside about 1¼ cups of the florets.

Heat 2 tablespoons of the margarine in a large soup pot. Add the onions, garlic, and celery and sauté over moderate heat until the onions are golden. Slowly sprinkle in the flour, stirring it in until it disappears. Add the chopped broccoli (except for the reserved florets), tomato, parsley, seasoning mix, and just enough stock or water to cover. Bring to a boil, then cover and simmer over low heat for 15 to 20 minutes, or until the broccoli is tender but not overdone. Remove from the heat.

Transfer the solid ingredients to the container of a food processor or blender with a slotted spoon and purée, in batches if necessary, until smooth. Stir back into the stock in the soup pot and add enough milk or soymilk to achieve a smooth and slightly thick consistency. Return to very low heat.

Cook the pasta in a separate saucepan in rapidly simmering water until it is *al dente.* Drain and rinse briefly under cool water. In the meantime, steam the broccoli florets until they are bright green and tender-crisp.

Heat the remaining tablespoon of margarine in a skillet. Sauté the pasta until it just begins to brown lightly. Stir the pasta and the steamed florets into the soup, then season to taste with salt and pepper. Let the soup remain on very low heat for another 5 minutes, then serve, garnishing each serving with some grated cheese.

To make nutritious, healthful, and palatable soup, with flavors properly commingled, is an art which requires study and practice, but it is surprising from what a scant allotment of material a delicate and appetizing dish may be produced.

—*The Buckeye Cookbook,* 1883

CHINESE CABBAGE AND BEAN CURD SOUP

4 to 6 servings

This light soup is a great introduction to a Chinese-style dinner. Serve Fried Scallion Logs (page 119) with it.

1 tablespoon peanut or safflower oil
1 large onion, quartered and thinly sliced
2 cups firmly packed, finely shredded savoy cabbage
¾ cup small, thinly sliced mushrooms
1 small white turnip, quartered and thinly sliced,
    or ⅓ cup sliced water chestnuts
1 recipe Onion or Leek and Garlic Broth (page 11),
    or Oriental Mushroom Broth (page 14)
2 tablespoons dry sherry or wine
2 teaspoons natural soy sauce
½ teaspoon lemon-pepper
1 cup snow peas, trimmed and halved
½ pound tofu (bean curd), cut into ½-inch dice

Heat the oil in a large soup pot. Add the onion and sauté over low heat until it is golden. Add the remaining ingredients, except the snow peas and tofu, bring to a boil, then cover and simmer over low heat for 10 minutes. Remove from the heat. Stir in the snow peas and tofu and let the soup stand for 30 minutes. Heat through as needed and serve at once.

MISO-SPINACH SOUP WITH BABY CORN

4 to 6 servings

A simple, quick and colorful soup, I devised this to make a modest quantity, since it is best eaten on the day that it is made (it will keep one more day if need be). This is a light introduction to an Oriental rice or noodle dish. For more information on miso, see page 12, under Simple Miso Broth.

1 tablespoon peanut oil
1 medium carrot, coarsely chopped
½ pound spinach, washed, stemmed,
    and coarsely chopped
3 scallions, white and green parts
1 recipe Basic Dashi (page 13), Light Vegetable Stock
    (page 10), or 5 cups water
2 to 3 tablespoons sherry or dry wine
¼ teaspoon lemon-pepper
¼ pound block tofu, cut into ½-inch dice
15- or 16-ounce can baby corn, cut into 1-inch pieces
2 to 4 tablespoons miso, to taste

Heat the oil in a large soup pot. Add the carrot and sauté over moderate heat for 2 minutes, stirring frequently. Add the spinach, scallions, liquid, sherry or wine, and lemon-pepper. Bring to a boil, then cover and simmer over very low heat for 10 minutes. Add the tofu and baby corn. Dissolve the miso in enough water to make it smooth and pourable. Stir it in, and simmer for another 5 minutes over very low heat. Serve at once.

EGGDROP NOODLE SOUP WITH EXOTIC MUSHROOMS

6 servings

For those who love unusual mushrooms, this Oriental-style soup will be a treat. Fried Scallion Logs (page 119) make a nice accompaniment. This is a perfect introduction to a simple dinner of stir-fried vegetables with tofu.

2 teaspoons sesame oil
1 clove garlic, minced
4 scallions, white and green parts, sliced
1 recipe Oriental Mushroom Broth (page 14)
Shiitake mushrooms from above broth,
    trimmed of tough stems and sliced
15- or 16-ounce can Oriental mushrooms, such as
    straw, abalone, or oyster mushrooms (leave straw
    mushrooms whole, coarsely chop abalone or oyster),
    including liquid
5- or 6-ounce can water chestnuts, including
    liquid, sliced
1 tablespoon rice vinegar
1 tablespoon cornstarch
4 ounces rice-stick noodles
Natural soy sauce to taste
Freshly ground pepper to taste
2 eggs, beaten

Heat the oil in a large soup pot, then add the garlic and white parts of the scallions and sauté over moderate heat for 2 or 3 minutes. Add the green parts of the scallions along with the broth, mushrooms, water chestnuts, and rice vinegar. Bring to a boil, then simmer over low heat, covered, for 10 minutes.

Dissolve the cornstarch in just enough water to make it pourable and stir into the soup. Break up the rice noodles and add them to the soup. Simmer for 5 minutes, or until the rice noodles are done. Season to taste with soy sauce and freshly ground pepper, and adjust the consistency with water if the soup looks like it needs a bit more liquid. Pour in the eggs in a thin, steady stream. Remove from the heat and serve at once.

I am a mushroom
On whom the dew of heaven
Drops now and then.

—John Ford (1586-1639)
  The Broken Heart

PARSLEY-POTATO SOUP

6 to 8 servings

Lots of fresh parsley and a bit of cream cheese are what give this soup its special character. A crusty French or Italian bread goes well with this soup.

2 tablespoons margarine
1 large onion, chopped
2 cloves garlic, minced
6 medium potatoes, peeled and diced
1 medium celery stalk, finely chopped
2 bay leaves
Light Vegetable Stock (page 10) or water
1½ teaspoons Italian herb seasoning mix
4 ounces cream cheese, diced
½ cup firmly packed chopped fresh parsley
¼ cup quick-cooking oats
1 cup low-fat milk, or as needed
Salt and freshly ground pepper to taste

Heat the margarine in a large soup pot. Add the onion and sauté over moderate heat until it is golden. Add the garlic, potatoes, celery, and bay leaves. Add enough stock or water to cover, then stir in the seasoning mix. Bring to a boil, then simmer over low heat, covered, until the potatoes are just tender, about 20 to 25 minutes.

Remove about ½ cup of the hot liquid and transfer it to a small mixing bowl. Combine with the cream cheese and whisk together until smooth and creamy. Stir into the soup along with the parsley. Slowly sprinkle in the oats. Simmer for another 20 to 25 minutes over very low heat, or until the potatoes are completely tender. Add the milk and season to taste with salt and pepper.

This soup thickens as it stands; thin as needed with additional milk, then correct the seasonings.

S·U·M·M·E·R

When the appetite is dulled by summer heat, there is nothing more appealing than a bowl of refreshing cold soup. These soups make lavish use of herbs, summer vegetables such as corn, and lush fruits. For really lazy, languid days, you will find a number of soups that require no cooking at all.

POTATO-SPINACH BUTTERMILK SOUP

6 to 8 servings

A cold soup that is substantial as well as refreshing.

5 to 6 medium potatoes, peeled and diced
1 small onion, cut in half
1 tablespoon margarine
2 bay leaves
Light Vegetable Stock (page 10) or water
1 pound fresh spinach leaves, well washed,
    stemmed, and chopped
1 cup steamed fresh or thawed frozen green peas
2 to 2½ cups buttermilk, as needed
2 to 3 tablespoons chopped fresh parsley
1 tablespoon chopped fresh dill
Salt and freshly ground pepper to taste

Place the first 4 ingredients in a large soup pot. Add just enough stock or water to cover. Bring to a boil, then cover and simmer over moderately low heat until the potatoes are tender, about 25 minutes. With a slotted spoon, remove and discard onion halves. Transfer a heaping cupful of the potato dice into a small bowl, mash well and stir back into the soup. Stir in the spinach leaves and allow the soup to cool to room temperature. Stir in the remaining ingredients and season to taste with salt and pepper. Chill the soup thoroughly before serving.

MIDDLE EASTERN CUCUMBER-YOGURT SOUP

4 to 6 servings

Here's an exceptionally easy no-cook soup—a classic from the Middle East. I prefer it with barley added, as suggested in the variation below.

2 large cucumbers, peeled and seeded
1 pint plain yogurt
¼ cup finely chopped fresh herbs (choose
    from among or combine dill, parsley, and mint)
1½ cups low-fat milk, or as needed
1 teaspoon granulated sugar
½ teaspoon ground cumin
Salt and freshly ground pepper to taste
Juice of ½ lemon, optional

Grate the cucumbers on a coarse grater, then place them in a colander. Place the colander over the container in which you will serve the soup. Salt the grated cucumbers lightly and let stand for 30 minutes. The juice from the cucumbers will drain into the container and the cucumbers themselves will get nice and crisp.

Place the cucumbers in the container with the cucumber juice. Stir in the yogurt, herbs, and enough milk to give a slightly thick consistency. Stir in the sugar and seasonings, then add the optional lemon juice if you'd like an extra-tangy flavor. Serve at once or refrigerate until needed.

Variation:
For a heartier version of this soup, add a cup or so of cold, cooked barley.

CREAM OF CORN AND WATERCRESS SOUP

6 to 8 servings

The peppery flavor of watercress provides an excellent contrast to the sweetness of summer corn.

6 medium ears fresh, sweet corn
2 tablespoons margarine
2 large onions, chopped
2 cloves garlic, minced
2 medium potatoes, diced
4 cups cooking liquid from the corn
2 cups chopped watercress leaves
   and stems, divided
1 teaspoon Italian herb seasoning mix
2 cups low-fat milk or soymilk, or as needed
Salt and freshly ground pepper to taste

Cook the corn in rapidly simmering water until done. Scoop out the ears and reserve the water. Allow to cool, and when cool enough to handle, scrape the kernels off the cob with a sharp knife. Set aside.

Heat the margarine in a large soup pot. Add the onion and garlic and sauté over moderate heat until golden. Add the potatoes and cooking liquid from the corn, and bring to a boil. Simmer over low heat, covered, for 10 minutes. Add half of the watercress along with the seasoning mix. Simmer until the potatoes are tender, about another 10 to 15 minutes, then remove from the heat.

Set aside a cup of the corn kernels, and purée the remainder in a food processor or blender until fairly smooth. Transfer to a bowl. With a slotted spoon, transfer the solid ingredients from the soup to the food processor or blender and purée in batches until smooth. Return the purée to the soup pot, along with the corn purée, the reserved corn kernels, and the reserved watercress. Return to low heat and stir in enough milk or soymilk to achieve a slightly thick consistency. Season to taste with salt and pepper, then cover and simmer over low heat for another 10 to 15 minutes. Let the soup cool to room temperature, then refrigerate until chilled.

"Eat well of the cresses" was a common bit of advice given by Renaissance herbalists, for it was believed that consuming these greens aided the memory.

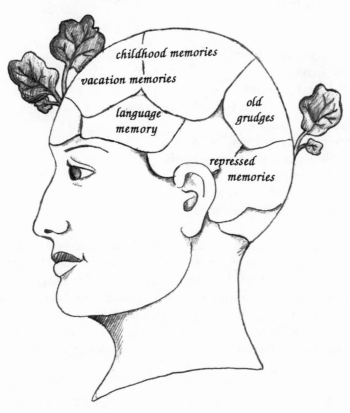

COLD ZUCCHINI AND CORN SOUP

6 to 8 servings

Zucchini and corn are an appealing team. Serve with Garlic Croutons (page 121) for a nice crunch.

2 tablespoons olive oil, divided
1 small onion, chopped
1 clove garlic, minced
2 pounds zucchini, diced
2 cups cooked fresh corn kernels (from about
   3 good-sized ears)
¾ cup chopped fresh parsley
5 cups Light Vegetable Stock (page 10) or water
1 teaspoon ground cumin
2 scallions, green parts only, minced
2 tablespoons finely chopped fresh basil
1 cup reduced-fat sour cream
1 to 2 tablespoons lemon juice, to taste
Salt and freshly ground pepper to taste

Heat half of the oil in a large soup pot. Add the onion and garlic and sauté over moderately low heat until the onion is golden. Set aside half of the zucchini dice and half of the corn kernels. Add the remaining half to the soup pot along with the parsley, stock or water, and cumin. Bring to a boil, then simmer, covered, over low heat until the zucchini is tender, about 10 minutes.

Transfer the solid ingredients to the container of a food processor and purée, in batches if necessary, until smooth. Return to the soup pot, then allow to cool to room temperature.

Heat the remaining olive oil in a skillet. Add the reserved zucchini and sauté over moderate heat until it is just beginning to brown lightly. When the soup is cool, stir in the sautéed zucchini, reserved corn kernels, scallions, basil, sour cream, and lemon juice. Correct the consistency if necessary with additional water or stock, then season to taste with salt and freshly ground pepper. Serve at room temperature or chilled, as you prefer.

> *Her hair that lay along her back*
> *Was yellow like ripe corn.*

—Dante Gabriel Rossetti (1828-82)
  The Blessed Damozel

CREAMY CORN SOUP WITH ROASTED PEPPERS

6 servings

Late summer is the time to make this soup, which looks as appealing as it tastes.

6 large ears fresh sweet corn
2 tablespoons margarine, divided
2 large onions, chopped
2 cloves garlic, minced
4 cups cooking liquid from the corn
Dash cayenne pepper
1 to 1½ cups low-fat milk or soymilk, as needed
Salt and freshly ground pepper to taste
2 large sweet red bell peppers
1 large green bell pepper
6 large fresh basil leaves,
    sliced into strips, optional

Cook the corn in rapidly simmering water until the kernels are just tender. Remove the ears with tongs (save the cooking water) and set on a plate until cool enough to handle. Then, scrape the kernels off the cobs with a sharp knife. Measure off 1 cup of kernels and set aside.

Heat half of the margarine in a large soup pot. Add the onions and garlic, and sauté over moderate heat until the onions are nicely golden, and just beginning to be touched with brown spots. Transfer to the container of a food processor and process with the corn kernels (except for the reserved cup), in batches if necessary, until quite smooth. Transfer back to the soup pot.

Stir in the cooking liquid from the corn and the reserved corn kernels. Bring to a simmer, then add the cayenne pepper and enough milk or soymilk to achieve a slightly thick consistency. Simmer over low heat, covered, for 10 minutes. Season to taste with salt and pepper. Allow the soup to stand off the heat for about an hour.

In the meantime, set the peppers under the broiler, turning them frequently until the skins are quite blistered and fairly charred. Place the peppers in a brown paper bag and fold shut. Let the peppers cool in the bag for 30 minutes or so, then remove them from the bag, slip the skins off, and remove stems and seeds. Cut the peppers into thin, 2-inch-long strips.

The soup should be served warm, but not hot, though it is also delicious at room temperature. Garnish each serving with the roasted pepper strips and basil leaves.

Pray let me an American, inform the gentleman, who seems ignorant of the matter, that Indian corn, take it all in all, is one of the most agreeable and wholesome grains in the world.

—Benjamin Franklin (1706-1790)

FRESH TOMATO SOUP WITH SWEET CORN SAUCE

6 servings

This unusual cold soup is quite elegant, and is as interesting to look at as it is to eat. Follow this soup with a pasta salad for a light summer meal.

2 pounds ripe, flavorful tomatoes
2 tablespoons olive oil
2 large onions, chopped
2 cloves garlic, minced
2 large celery stalks, diced
1 medium potato, scrubbed and finely diced
¼ cup chopped fresh basil
2 tablespoons chopped fresh dill
1 teaspoon salt-free herb-and-spice seasoning mix
4 ears fresh corn
½ cup sour cream or yogurt, or a mixture
1½ to 2 cups tomato juice, as needed
1 tablespoon lemon juice
Salt and freshly ground pepper to taste
Chopped fresh basil for garnish

Bring 8 cups of water to a boil in a large pot. Place the whole tomatoes in the boiling water, remove from the heat, and let stand for 1 minute. Remove the tomatoes, and when they are cool enough to handle, peel them. Chop and set aside.

Heat the oil in a large soup pot. Add the onions, garlic, and celery and sauté over moderate heat, stirring frequently, until the onion is golden. Add the potato, the chopped tomatoes, and 2 cups of water. Bring to a boil, then simmer over low heat, covered, until the potato is tender, about 20 minutes. Add the basil, dill, and seasoning mix and simmer for another 5 minutes. Remove from the heat and allow to cool to room temperature.

In the meantime, cook the corn and allow it to cool. Once cool enough to handle, scrape off the kernels with a sharp knife. Combine the corn kernels with the sour cream or yogurt in the container of a food processor or blender and purée until velvety smooth. Place in a container and refrigerate until needed.

Once the soup mixture has cooled, purée it in batches in a food processor or blender until smooth. Return it to the soup pot and add enough tomato juice to achieve a smooth and slightly thick consistency. Stir in the lemon juice and season to taste with salt and pepper. Refrigerate until chilled.

To serve, fill each serving bowl about ¾ full with the tomato soup. Place a ladleful of the sweet corn sauce in the center of each bowl and garnish each serving with a sprinkling of chopped basil.

CARROT-YOGURT SOUP WITH BROCCOLI

6 to 8 servings

2 tablespoons margarine
2 large onions, chopped
1 pound carrots, thinly sliced
1 large potato, finely diced
2 large celery stalks, finely diced
2 large ripe tomatoes, chopped
2 bay leaves
2 teaspoons salt-free herb-and-spice seasoning mix
1 large bunch broccoli, finely chopped
1 cup plain yogurt
1 cup low-fat milk, or as needed
3 to 4 tablespoons minced fresh dill
½ teaspoon lemon-pepper
Salt to taste

Heat the margarine in a large soup pot. Add the onions and sauté over moderate heat until they are golden. Add the carrots, potato, celery, and tomatoes. Add just enough water to cover, and stir in the bay leaves and seasoning mix. Bring to a boil, then simmer over low heat, covered, until all the vegetables are tender, about 25 minutes. Remove the bay leaves. Allow the soup to cool to room temperature. Purée the soup, in batches, in a food processor or blender.

Steam the broccoli until bright green and tender-crisp. Stir it into the soup followed by the yogurt and enough milk to achieve a slightly thick consistency. Stir in the dill and lemon-pepper, season to taste with salt, and serve.

GARDEN GREENS SOUP

6 servings

2 tablespoons safflower oil
2 medium onions, quartered and thinly sliced
1 large celery stalk, finely diced
½ small head savoy cabbage, finely shredded
¼ cup oatmeal
12 ounces spinach, washed, stemmed, and chopped
2 cups shredded lettuce, any dark green variety
2 medium tomatoes, finely diced
¼ cup chopped fresh parsley
2 tablespoons minced fresh dill
2 bunches scallions, thinly sliced
½ teaspoon good quality curry powder or *garam masala*
1 tablespoon white wine or balsamic vinegar
1½ cups buttermilk, or as needed
Salt and freshly ground pepper to taste

Heat the oil in a large soup pot. Add the onion and celery and sauté over moderate heat until the onion is golden. Add the cabbage, oatmeal, and 5 cups of water. Bring to a boil, then simmer, covered, over low heat for 10 minutes. Add the spinach, lettuce, tomatoes, parsley, dill, scallions, curry powder, and vinegar. Simmer over low heat for 10 minutes, then remove from the heat. Allow the soup to cool to room temperature.

Stir in the buttermilk as needed, to achieve a slightly thick consistency. Season to taste with salt and pepper. Refrigerate the soup for an hour or so before serving.

CREAM OF LETTUCE SOUP

6 servings

Cheddar-Oat Griddle Biscuits (page 114) provide a nice contrast to the mild flavor of this pleasant summer soup.

2 tablespoons margarine
2 medium onions, chopped
3 to 4 cloves garlic, minced
10 cups coarsely chopped lettuce, divided
1 cup low-fat milk
Juice of ½ lemon
3 tablespoons minced fresh herbs (choose from a
    mixture of chives, dill, oregano, basil)
⅔ cup yogurt
Salt and lemon-pepper to taste

Heat the margarine in a large soup pot. Add the onions and garlic and sauté over moderate heat until the onions are lightly browned. Add 2½ cups of water and 8 cups of the lettuce, reserving the rest. Bring to a boil, then simmer over low heat, covered, for 20 minutes. With a slotted spoon, transfer the solid ingredients to the container of a food processor or blender, and purée, in batches if necessary, until smooth.

Return to the soup pot or to a serving tureen. Stir in the milk, lemon juice, and herbs. Allow to cool to room temperature. Stir in the yogurt, and if the soup is too thick, add a bit more milk. Season to taste with salt and lemon-pepper.

Finely shred the reserved lettuce and steam it in a small saucepan, covered, just until wilted. Stir into the soup. Refrigerate the soup for at least an hour before serving. This soup is best fresh, eaten the same day it is made.

CREAMY AVOCADO SOUP

4 to 6 servings

A quick and easy no-cook soup, this is remarkably refreshing on a hot summer day. It's best eaten on the same day as it is make, since avocado discolors and does not keep well under refrigeration once opened.

2 large, ripe avocados
Juice of ½ lemon
1½ cups buttermilk
1¼ to 1½ cups low-fat milk
1 medium green or red bell pepper, finely chopped
2 scallions, green parts only, sliced into fine rings
2 tablespoons finely chopped fresh dill
2 tablespoons finely chopped fresh parsley
½ teaspoon ground cumin
½ teaspoon good quality curry powder or *garam masala*
Salt and freshly ground pepper to taste

Mash 1½ avocados well, and finely dice the remaining half. Place all in a serving container, and mix immediately with the lemon juice. Stir in the buttermilk, and enough milk to achieve a slightly thick consistency. Stir in the remaining ingredients and refrigerate, covered, until thoroughly chilled.

GAZPACHO

6 servings

A collection of vegetarian soups would be incomplete without this Spanish classic.

The base:
14-ounce can plum tomatoes with liquid
⅔ large cucumber, cut into chunks
⅔ large green or red bell pepper, cut into chunks
2 bunches scallions, cut into several pieces
Handful of parsley sprigs
1 tablespoon chopped fresh dill, or 1 teaspoon dried dill

To finish the soup:
3 cups tomato juice, or as needed
⅓ large cucumber, finely diced
⅓ large green or red bell pepper, finely diced
2 fresh plum tomatoes, finely diced
1 large carrot, finely diced
1 medium celery stalk, finely diced
Juice of ½ to 1 lemon, to taste
2 teaspoons chili powder, or to taste
Salt and freshly ground pepper to taste

Garlic Croutons (page 121) for topping, optional

Place all the ingredients for the soup base in the container of a food processor or blender. Purée until fairly smooth. Transfer the purée to a serving container. Stir in enough tomato juice to give the soup a slightly thick consistency. Add the remaining ingredients. Stir together, then cover and refrigerate for at least an hour before serving. If desired, top each serving with the optional croutons.

SWEET-AND-SOUR RED CABBAGE SOUP

6 to 8 servings

This refreshing soup is reminiscent of a cold beet borscht. A food processor will make all the grating easier, though the cabbage may be shredded by hand.

1 medium onion, quartered and thinly sliced or grated
2 medium apples, peeled, cored, and grated
1 large carrot, grated
¾ small head red cabbage, finely shredded
2 cups apple juice
¼ cup apple cider vinegar
¼ cup dry red wine
3 tablespoons brown sugar, or to taste
1 teaspoon salt, or to taste
Sour cream, or a mixture of half sour cream
   and half yogurt, optional

Place the first 5 ingredients in a large soup pot along with enough water to cover. As the liquid is coming to a boil, add the vinegar, wine, and brown sugar. Simmer over low heat, covered, until the vegetables are tender, about 40 minutes. Stir in the salt, and allow the soup to cool to room temperature. Refrigerate the soup for at least an hour before serving. Top each serving with a scoop of sour cream or sour cream-yogurt mixture, if you'd like.

An idealist is one who, on noticing that a rose smells better than a cabbage, concludes that it will also make a better soup.

—H.L. Mencken (1880-1956)
Chrestomantry

SPICED SUMMER FRUIT SOUP

6 or more servings

This is the only one of the fruit soups given here that needs a bit of cooking. The wine and spices give it a lovely flavor.

1 medium sweet apple, peeled, cored,
    and finely diced
½ pint blueberries
2 plums, diced
3 medium peaches, diced
1 cup seedless red or green grapes
1 cup hulled and chopped strawberries
Juice of ½ lemon
4½ cups apple juice
2-inch stick cinnamon
5 whole cloves
⅓ cup semisweet red wine
4 to 5 tablespoons light brown sugar, to taste

Combine all the ingredients in a large soup pot. Bring to a boil, then simmer over low heat, covered, for 20 to 25 minutes, until the fruit is tender. Allow the soup to cool, then refrigerate until chilled. If the soup is too dense, adjust the consistency with more apple juice.

He that would have the fruit must climb the tree.

—Thomas Fuller
Gnomologia, 1732

STRAWBERRY-BUTTERMILK SOUP

6 servings

This super-quick no-cook soup is delicious enough to serve as dessert.

1 quart ripe, sweet strawberries, washed, hulled,
** and cut into approximately ½-inch chunks**
1 cup apple juice
2 cups buttermilk
¼ cup dry red wine
3 to 4 tablespoons honey, or to taste
¼ teaspoon cinnamon
Fresh mint leaves for garnish, optional

Crush a scant cup of the strawberries, then combine them with the cut strawberries and the remaining ingredients, except for the mint leaves, in a serving container. Refrigerate for an hour or so before serving. If desired, garnish each serving with a few mint leaves.

The man in the wilderness asked of me,
How many strawberries grew in the sea.
I answered him, as I thought good,
As many as herrings grow in the wood.

—Mother Goose

CHILLED MELON SOUP

6 servings

It takes minutes to make this sweet soup. Try serving it after a meal, rather than before—it's a wonderful palate cooler after a spicy meal.

**8 heaping cups lushly ripe cantaloupe or
   honeydew melon chunks, or half of each
1½ cups freshly squeezed orange juice
Juice of ½ to 1 lemon, to taste
3 to 5 tablespoons honey to taste, depending on sweetness
   of fruit
¼ cup semi-dry white wine
Dash each: cinnamon, nutmeg
1 cup strawberries, halved and sliced
Mint leaves for garnish, optional**

Set aside about 2 cups of the melon chunks, and place the rest in the container of a food processor or blender. Process until smoothly puréed, then add the orange and lemon juice, honey, wine, and spices. Process again until thoroughly blended. Transfer the mixture to a serving container.

Cut the reserved melon chunks into ½-inch dice and stir them into the soup along with the strawberries. Cover and chill for at least an hour before serving. Garnish each serving with 2 or 3 mint leaves if desired.

Friends are like melons,
Shall I tell you why?
To find one good
You must a hundred try.

—Claude Mermet, 1600

MINTED PEACHES-AND-CREAM SOUP

6 servings

2½ pounds ripe, juicy peaches
1 cup freshly squeezed orange juice
1 cup apple juice
1 cup light cream
1 teaspoon vanilla extract
½ teaspoon ground ginger
Dash of nutmeg
2 tablespoons crushed fresh mint leaves, or
    1 mint tea bag
½ cup boiling water

Cut the peaches away from their pits in chunks. Reserve about 2 cups, and place the rest in the container of a food processor or blender, along with the juices, cream, vanilla, and spices. Process until smoothly puréed, then transfer to a serving container.

In a cup or small bowl, steep the fresh mint or mint tea in the boiling water for 10 to 15 minutes. Stir into the peach soup along with the reserved peaches, then refrigerate for an hour or two to allow the flavors to blend. Before serving, stir the soup, and adjust the consistency if necessary with more apple or orange juice.

A·C·C·O·M·P·A·N·I-M·E·N·T·S

Here is a selection of quick breads, muffins, scones, dumplings, and the like that you can make to accompany your soups. Most are very easy, and should ideally be made while the soup is simmering, so that they can be served fresh and warm.

QUICK SUNFLOWER-CHEESE BREAD

Makes 1 loaf

This tasty bread goes well with many soups, but is especially good with mixed vegetable soups and tomato-based soups.

2 cups whole wheat pastry flour
2 teaspoons baking powder
½ teaspoon salt
2 eggs, well beaten
½ cup low-fat milk or soymilk
¼ cup melted margarine
2 tablespoons honey
1 teaspoon prepared mustard
1 cup firmly packed grated Cheddar cheese
   or Cheddar-style soy cheese
3 tablespoons toasted sunflower seeds

Preheat the oven to 350 degrees.

Combine the first 3 ingredients in a mixing bowl. In another bowl, beat together the eggs, milk or soymilk, melted margarine, honey, and mustard. Combine the wet ingredients with the dry, stirring vigorously until thoroughly mixed. Stir in the cheese and sunflower seeds.

Pour the batter into a lightly oiled 5 by 9 by 3-inch loaf pan. Bake for 45 minutes, or until the top looks golden brown and crusty. When the loaf pan is cool enough to handle, remove the loaf, place it on a rack, and allow it to cool somewhat before slicing.

FOCACCIA BREAD

Makes 1 round loaf

Although this excellent traditional Italian bread is yeasted, it does not take as long to make as other yeasted breads, since it only requires one rather brief rising. If you are making a long-simmering soup, this bread will likely fit into the time frame.

1 package active dry yeast
1 cup warm water
1 tablespoon light brown sugar
¼ cup olive oil, divided
1½ cups whole wheat flour
1 cup unbleached white flour
1 teaspoon salt
Garlic powder
Coarse salt
Dried oregano or rosemary

Pour the yeast into the warm water and let stand to dissolve for 5 to 10 minutes. Stir in the brown sugar and half of the olive oil. In a large mixing bowl, combine the flours and salt. Work the yeast mixture in, using your hands, then turn out onto a well-floured board. Knead for 5 minutes, adding additional flour if the dough is too sticky. Shape into a round and roll out into a circle with a 12-inch diameter. Cover with a tea towel and let rise in a warm place for 30 to 40 minutes. With your fingers, poke shallow holes all over the top at even intervals. Pour the remaining olive oil over the top evenly, then sprinkle with the garlic powder, coarse salt, and herbs.

Bake in a preheated 400-degree oven for 20 to 25 minutes, or until the bread is golden on top and sounds hollow when tapped. Cut into wedges to serve, or just break pieces off. Serve warm.

WHOLE WHEAT VEGETABLE MUFFINS

Makes 1 dozen

Tiny bits of fresh vegetables give these muffins a very special flavor and texture. They are particularly good with puréed soups and cheese soups.

1 cup assorted fresh vegetables,
  cut into approximately 1-inch chunks
  (choose from among carrot, green pepper,
  radish, cabbage, and zucchini)
1 egg, beaten
¼ cup safflower or vegetable oil
2 tablespoons honey
½ cup low-fat milk or soymilk
1 teaspoon finely grated onion
1½ cups whole wheat flour
½ cup unbleached white flour
1½ teaspoons baking powder
½ teaspoon salt
Poppy seeds for topping, optional

Preheat the oven to 350 degrees.

Place the vegetable chunks in a food processor. Pulse on and off until the vegetables are very finely minced. They should measure about 1 cup. Set aside. In a mixing bowl, combine the beaten egg with the oil, honey, milk or soymilk, and onion. Stir together and add the minced vegetables.

In another bowl, combine the flours, baking powder, and salt. Add the wet ingredients to the dry, and stir together until well blended. Divide the mixture among 12 oiled or paper-lined muffin tins. Top with the optional poppy seeds. Bake for 20 to 25 minutes, or until the tops are golden brown. Remove the muffins from the tins as soon as they are cool enough to handle and cool them on a rack or a plate.

CHEESE AND HERB CORN MUFFINS

Makes 1 dozen

Moist and flavorful, these muffins are especially nice with bean soups.

⅔ cup cornmeal
1 cup whole wheat pastry flour
1 teaspoon baking powder
½ teaspoon baking soda
½ teaspoon salt
1½ teaspoons mixed dried herbs of your choice
1 egg, beaten
¼ cup safflower or vegetable oil
1 cup buttermilk
1 cup grated cheese, any white or yellow cheese
   of your choice

Preheat the oven to 375 degrees.

Combine the first 6 ingredients in a mixing bowl. In another bowl, combine the beaten egg with the oil and buttermilk. Combine the wet and dry ingredients, and stir until thoroughly mixed. Stir in the grated cheese. Divide the batter among 12 lightly oiled or paper-lined muffin tins. Bake for 15 minutes, or until golden brown and a toothpick inserted into the center of one tests clean. Cool on a rack, then store in an airtight container as soon as the muffins are at room temperature.

Five muffins are enough for any man at a meal.

—E.V. Knox (1881-1971)
   Gorgeous Times

BUTTERMILK OAT MUFFINS

Makes 1 dozen

Mild and just slightly sweet, these are good teamed with spicy or highly textured soups.

1¼ cups whole wheat flour
¾ cup rolled oats
1½ teaspoons baking powder
½ teaspoon baking soda
½ teaspoon salt
1 egg, beaten
¾ cup buttermilk
3 tablespoons honey
¼ cup safflower or vegetable oil

Preheat the oven to 350 degrees.

Combine the first 5 ingredients in a mixing bowl. In another bowl, beat together the remaining 4 ingredients. Slowly pour the wet ingredients into the dry and stir vigorously until thoroughly combined. Distribute among 12 oiled or paper-lined muffin tins. Bake for 15 to 20 minutes, or until golden brown and a toothpick inserted into the center of one tests clean.

BARLEY OR RICE TRIANGLES

Makes about 20 to 22

These offbeat little breads, made on a griddle, go very nicely with bean soups, cheese soups, and puréed soups.

1¼ cups whole wheat pastry flour
¼ cup cornmeal
1 teaspoon baking powder
1 teaspoon salt
3 tablespoons margarine, softened
1 cup well-cooked barley or brown rice
¼ cup low-fat milk or soymilk, or as needed

Combine the first 4 ingredients in a mixing bowl and stir together. Cut the margarine into bits and blend into the flour mixture with the tines of a fork or a pastry blender until the mixture resembles coarse crumbs. Stir in the cooked barley or rice, then add enough milk or soymilk so that the mixture adheres as a firm dough, working it together with your hands.

Divide the dough into 2 parts. On a well-floured board, roll out 1 part until it is ¼ inch thick. With a sharp knife, cut the dough into triangular pieces with approximately 2-inch sides. Repeat with the remaining dough, gathering up any dough left over from cutting and rolling out again until it is all used up.

Heat a griddle or large nonstick skillet. Bake the triangles over moderate heat until they are touched with light brown on both sides. Transfer to a plate to cool, and once they are at room temperature, keep them in a covered container.

CHEDDAR-OAT GRIDDLE BISCUITS

Makes about 20

The sharp Cheddar cheese contrasts well with mild-flavored soups.

1 cup whole wheat pastry flour
1 cup rolled oats
1 teaspoon salt
1 teaspoon baking powder
¼ cup margarine, softened
1 cup grated sharp Cheddar cheese or Cheddar-style soy cheese
¼ cup low-fat milk or soymilk, as needed

Combine the first 4 ingredients in a mixing bowl. Cut the margarine into bits, then work into the flour-oat mixture with the tines of a fork or a pastry blender until the mixture resembles coarse crumbs. Stir in the Cheddar cheese, then add enough milk to form a stiff dough, using your hands to work it together. Turn out onto a well-floured board, and roll the dough out to ¼-inch thickness. Cut the dough into 2-inch rounds using a cookie cutter or a glass. Gather up leftover dough and roll out again until all the dough is used up.

Heat a griddle or a large nonstick skillet and bake the biscuits on both sides over moderate heat until golden brown. Cool on a plate, then transfer to a covered container when cooled to room temperature.

Toasted cheese hath no master.

—John Ray
English Proverbs, 1670

POTATO-RYE GRIDDLE BISCUITS

Makes 16 to 18

These are especially good with soups containing beets, cabbage, or strong greens.

1 cup dark rye flour
¾ cup unbleached white flour
1 teaspoon baking powder
1 teaspoon salt
1 teaspoon caraway seeds, optional
1 cup well-mashed cooked potato, chilled
1 egg, beaten
¼ cup safflower or vegetable oil

Combine the first 5 ingredients in a mixing bowl. In another bowl, stir the remaining ingredients together. Work the wet ingredients into the dry, first with a spoon and then with your hands, to form a smooth, soft dough. Add just a bit more flour if the dough seems too sticky to handle. Divide the dough into 3 or 4 parts and roll each out to ¼-inch thickness on a floured board. Cut with the rim of a 2-inch round glass or cookie cutter. Knead together the leftover parts of the dough and roll out again until it is all used up.

Heat a lightly greased griddle. Bake each round for 5 to 7 minutes on each side, or until nicely golden. Serve warm.

ONION-RYE OVEN SCONES

Makes 8 scones

Moist and slightly crumbly, these scones team especially well with soups made of root vegetables—potatoes, parsnips, and the like.

1½ cups dark rye flour
¾ cup unbleached white flour
2 teaspoons baking powder
1 teaspoon salt
¼ cup margarine, softened
2 eggs, beaten
2 tablespoons molasses or honey
¼ cup low-fat milk or soymilk, or as needed

Topping:
1 tablespoon safflower oil
1 medium onion, quartered and thinly sliced
Poppy seeds

Preheat the oven to 350 degrees.

Combine the first 4 ingredients in a mixing bowl. Cut the margarine into the flour mixture with a pastry blender or the tines of a fork until the mixture resembles coarse crumbs.

In another bowl, combine the eggs and molasses or honey. Work into the flour mixture, followed by enough milk or soymilk to form a soft dough. Transfer the dough to a well-floured board and knead briefly with floured hands. Roll into a round 9 inches in diameter and place on a lightly oiled baking sheet. Score the round with a knife, about halfway through the dough, into 8 equal wedge-shaped parts.

For the topping, heat the oil in a small skillet. Add the onion and sauté over moderate heat until it is lightly browned. Distribute it evenly over the scones, then sprinkle with poppy seeds. Bake for 12 to 15 minutes, or until the top is golden. Let cool somewhat before slicing.

Sow timely thy white wheat, sow rye in the dust,
Let seed have his longing, let soil have her lust.
Let rye be partaken of Michelmas spring,
To bear out the hardness that winter doth bring.

—Thomas Tusser
Five Hundred Points of Good Husbandry, 1580

CURRANT GRIDDLE SCONES

8 servings

If you'd like an accompaniment to fruit soups, these slightly sweet scones are just the thing.

1½ cups whole wheat pastry flour
1½ teaspoons baking powder
¼ teaspoon cinnamon
¼ cup margarine, softened
¼ cup light brown sugar
¼ cup low-fat milk or soymilk, or as needed
⅔ cup dried currants
3 tablespoons finely chopped walnuts

In a mixing bowl, combine the flour with the baking powder and cinnamon. Cut the margarine into bits, then work into the flour with a pastry blender or the tines of a fork until the mixture resembles coarse crumbs. Stir in the brown sugar, then add enough milk or soymilk to hold the dough together. It should be a light, yet non-sticky dough. Work the currants and walnuts in with your hands, then turn the dough out onto a well floured board and knead briefly.

Form the dough into a ball, then roll out into a round, about 10 inches in diameter and ½-inch thick. Cut into 8 even pie-wedge shapes, then arrange on a heated griddle. Bake on both sides over moderate heat, about 8 to 10 minutes per side, or until golden brown. Cool on a rack, and serve warm at once.

FRIED SCALLION LOGS

Makes about 20

I devised these little breads as an accompaniment to light, Oriental-style soups.

1½ cups whole wheat pastry flour
1 tablespoon sesame seeds
½ teaspoon baking powder
1 egg, beaten
3 tablespoons safflower or vegetable oil
1 tablespoon natural soy sauce
2 scallions, minced
Oil for frying

Combine the flour, sesame seeds, and baking powder in a mixing bowl. In a small mixing bowl, combine the beaten egg with the oil, soy sauce, and scallions. Work the wet and dry mixtures together, using the hands toward the end to form a stiff dough. Turn out onto a well-floured board. With floured hands, tear off small bits of dough and roll between the palms to make finger-shaped logs, about 3 inches long.

Heat enough oil to coat the bottom of a heavy skillet. Gently arrange the logs in the skillet and fry them, turning on all sides until golden brown. Drain on paper towels. When they have cooled to room temperature, store them in a covered container.

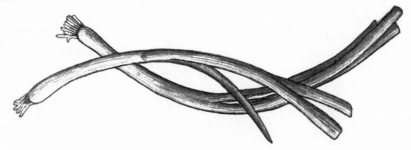

PARMESAN PITA WEDGES

Here s a really quick-to-fix idea, yielding good results with little effort. These are especially appropriate with Italian-style soups.

Pita bread (store-bought), preferably whole wheat,
   allowing 1 pita per serving
Extra-virgin olive oil
Freshly grated Parmesan cheese
Dried oregano, optional

Preheat the oven to 350 degrees.

Cut each pita into 4 wedges. Arrange on 1 or 2 baking sheets and brush the tops with olive oil. Sprinkle with Parmesan cheese and optional oregano. Bake for 5 minutes. Serve at once with hot soup.

Bread made from pure wheat flour... finely moulded and baked, comforteth and strengtheneth the heart, and maketh a man fat, and preserveth health.

—William Vaughn
   Directions for Health, 1600

GARLIC CROUTONS

This idea is so easy that it scarcely qualifies as a recipe, yet there are few embellishments for soup that are as simple, and that seem to please everyone so much. It's also a good way to use up bread that may otherwise go stale.

Ends and pieces of bread, several days old,
   allowing about 1 small slice per serving
1 clove garlic, cut in half lengthwise

Rub each piece of bread on both sides with the open side of the garlic clove. Cut the bread into approximately ½-inch dice. Discard the garlic or use for another purpose.

There are two ways in which to prepare the croutons. They may be arranged on a baking sheet and baked in a 275-degree oven for 20 minutes or so, until dry and crisp, then allowed to cool. Or, if the weather is warm and you don't wish to run the oven, simply toast the croutons in a heavy skillet over moderate heat, stirring frequently, about 20 minutes, or until dry and crisp.

Allow to cool. The croutons may be used once they have cooled, but if you can leave them out at room temperature for at least 30 minutes or so, they'll stay crisper in soup.

PARSLEY-POTATO DUMPLINGS

Makes 14 to 16 dumplings

If you've never made dumplings, you'll be surprised at how easy they are to make. They add substance and textural contrast to many types of soup.

⅔ cup whole wheat flour
⅔ cup unbleached white flour
1 teaspoon salt
1 cup cooked, well-mashed potatoes, chilled
1 egg, beaten
3 tablespoons minced fresh parsley

Combine the flours and salt in a mixing bowl. In another bowl, combine the mashed potatoes, egg, and parsley. Work the wet and dry ingredients together and shape into balls about l inch in diameter.

Bring water to a rolling boil in a large, heavy saucepan. Carefully drop the dumplings in. If they seem to stick to the bottom, gently nudge them with a wooden spoon. Cook at a steady simmer for 15 minutes, then drain. Serve hot with soup.

Never cut parsley if you are in love. If you give it away, you also give away your luck.

—Old European folk-belief

OAT-CHIVE DUMPLINGS

Makes 14 to 16 dumplings

⅔ cup fine oatmeal
⅔ cup unbleached white flour
2 tablespoons wheat germ
1 teaspoon salt
1 egg, beaten
1 tablespoon vegetable oil
2 tablespoons finely snipped chives
Several grindings of pepper
2 to 3 tablespoons milk or soymilk

Combine the oatmeal, flour, wheat germ, and salt in a mixing bowl. Beat the egg together with the oil, chives, and pepper, then work into the oatmeal mixture. Add enough milk or soymilk to form a stiff dough. Shape into balls about ¾ inch in diameter.

Bring water to a rolling boil in a large, deep, heavy saucepan. Carefully drop each dumpling in and cook at a steady simmer for 15 minutes. Drain and serve hot in soup.

CORNMEAL DUMPLINGS

Makes about 20 to 22

⅔ cup cornmeal
⅔ cup whole wheat pastry flour
1 teaspoon baking powder
1 teaspoon salt
Freshly ground pepper to taste
2 eggs, beaten
2 tablespoons safflower oil
4 to 5 tablespoons water

Combine the first 4 ingredients in a mixing bowl, then add a few grindings of pepper. In another bowl, beat the eggs together with the oil. Work the egg mixture into the flour mixture, then add just enough water to make the mixture adhesive, but not too loose.

Bring plenty of water to a full, rolling boil in a large saucepan. In the meantime, form the batter into approximately ¾-inch balls. When the water is boiling, gently drop them in. Allow them to cook at a medium simmer for 15 minutes, then remove with a slotted spoon. These may be served in soup at once, or cooled and refrigerated, and warmed up in a soup when needed.

INDEX